EYOTS AND AITS

EYOTS AND AITS
ISLANDS OF THE RIVER THAMES

MIRANDA VICKERS

The
History
Press

*This book is dedicated to my cousin Christine Contreras
with whom I shared such wonderful times as a child playing on Chiswick Eyot,
and to my husband John Maguire for his thorough reading and improvement of the text and
masterful command of the boat.*

First published 2012

The History Press
The Mill, Brimscombe Port
Stroud, Gloucestershire, GL5 2QG
www.thehistorypress.co.uk

© Miranda Vickers, 2012

The right of Miranda Vickers to be identified as the Author
of this work has been asserted in accordance with the
Copyrights, Designs and Patents Act 1988.

British Library Cataloguing in Publication Data.
A catalogue record for this book is available from the British Library.

ISBN 978 0 7524 6213 4

Typesetting and origination by The History Press
Printed in India
Manufacturing managed by Jellyfish Print Solutions Ltd

CONTENTS

ACKNOWLEDGEMENTS

IT HAS BEEN quite a difficult task finding information about the Thames islands because so little appears to have been written about them, so I am particularly grateful to the following people for their contributions to this book: to Suleman Akhtar for his help with Ash Island, Roger Mathias for information on Trowlock Island , Colin Reynolds for information about his lovely home, Rose Island, and Kevin Ella for help with Wheatley's Ait.

I am also grateful to Dan Van Der Vat and Michele Whitby for having written such a wonderful book on Eel Pie Island and particularly to Michele for providing her photos and imparting such great enthusiasm for this very special island. I would also like to thank the staff of Chiswick and Maidenhead Local Studies libraries for their kind assistance. Lastly, I want to thank Denis Harrison, for sharing with me his love of the River Thames and for ferrying me around the environs of Henley-on-Thames.

I owe a specific debt to the authors of the very few publications that specifically mention the Thames islands. Aside from the aforementioned *Eel Pie Island* (Francis Lincoln Ltd, 2009), foremost is Fred Thacker, the noted author of two of the most important books on the Thames, which have been extremely helpful, namely *The Thames Highway, A General History* (London 1914) and *The Thames Highway, Locks and Weirs* (London 1920). Also, Rowland Baker's *Thameside Molesey* has been invaluable. I am also indebted to the Sunbury and Shepperton Local History Society for their fascinating booklet 'Shepperton's Island Dwellers', which remains the only publication to date to chronicle the pioneer settlements on the Thames islands.

PHOTOGRAPHS & ILLUSTRATIONS

THE FOLLOWING PHOTOGRAPHS and illustrations have been reproduced with the kind permission of:
Chiswick Local Studies Library (pp.9, 20, 21, 22, 23, 24); Richmond Local Studies Library (pp. 39, 43, 62); Michele Whitby (pp.42, 45, 46); Kingston Local Studies Library (pp.51, 55); John Drewett (Vanity Fair, p.55); Andrew Cook (Maundy Gregory photographs on p.56); Suleman Akhtar (Ash Island around 1950 and the original Molesey Boat Club building on Ash Island pp.59, 60, 68); Tagg's Island Residents' Association (p.61); Monkey Island Hotel Ltd (p.101); and Maidenhead Local History Library (p.103). All other photographs by Miranda Vickers.

MAP OF THE THAMES

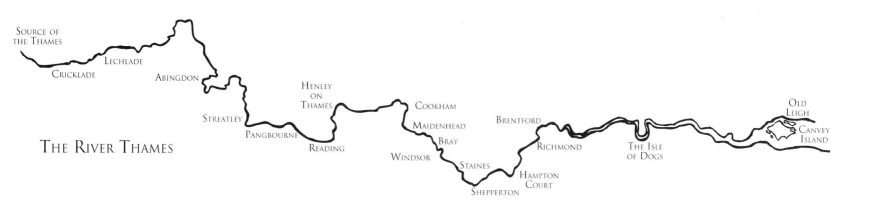

SOURCE OF
THE THAMES

LECHLADE

CRICKLADE

ABINGDON

STREATLEY

PANGBOURNE

READING

HENLEY
ON
THAMES

COOKHAM

MAIDENHEAD

BRAY

WINDSOR

STAINES

SHEPPERTON

HAMPTON
COURT

BRENTFORD

RICHMOND

THE ISLE
OF DOGS

OLD
LEIGH

CANVEY
ISLAND

THE RIVER THAMES

INTRODUCTION

As historian A.P. Herbert recalled, there are almost as many books about the River Thames as there are about love. And why not, given that this 'liquid history'[1] charts the story of Britain as it flows from the misty, windswept marshlands of the estuary, through London's teeming metropolis, and on to the lush, tranquil water meadows of Oxfordshire. These books describe every imaginable aspect of the Thames from its bridges, tunnels, weirs and locks, to its boatyards and boathouses. But surprisingly as yet no publication has covered the 190 or so islands spread along the river's 215-mile course from source to sea.

The islands are known as eyots, pronounced 'aits', a term that is used almost exclusively for islands in the River Thames. The word 'eyot' is derived from the old English term 'igeth', which is based on 'ieg', later corrupted to 'ey', meaning a small island. Despite eyot and ait meaning the same thing, islands are named very specifically with either one or the other, such as Chiswick Eyot or Garrick's Ait. Looking at early maps of the river, it is strikingly apparent that there used to be many more islands than there are today. For example, a map of the Thames at Maidenhead in 1637 depicts a total of twenty-two islands, whereas today the same stretch of river contains just twelve islands.[2] Over time some have silted up and joined the mainland bank; others have either been eroded by the flow of the river or dredged away to aid navigation.

Most of the Thames islands were formed naturally but some have been artificially created by the construction of lock cuts or the re-routing of navigation channels. The majority of islands, especially those on bends, were created over many centuries through the action of silt and debris accumulating around outcrops of chalk on the river bed or on gravel bars at the tail of a particularly fast stretch of water. Centuries ago the Thames was much lower and wider than it is now, and the contour of the river was continually changing. As Thames historian Sydney Dutton explains, instead of being confined within its regular banks, the parent river with its numerous tributaries spread its sluggish waters over many lagoons and flood plains, which were dotted here and there with islands of varying shapes and sizes. This is indicated by the fact that the word 'ey' enters into the composition of names of many riverside towns and villages such as Bermondsey, Putney, Molesey, Chertsey, Boveney or Henley – all of which may have once been islands in the Thames Valley lagoons.[3]

The tidal Thames islands stand noticeably higher above water level than the non-tidal islands. This is due to the large-scale dumping of waste material upon the islands over the past three and a half centuries. After the Great Fire of London in 1666, Berkshire stone was brought upriver in barges for the rebuilding of the city. On their return journey, the barges carried rubble to be dumped on the islands. Later, in the nineteenth century, during the huge excavations for the London underground and sewage systems, thousands of tons of rubble and soil were also dumped on the islands nearest to central London. This gave the islands solid foundations, and raised them high enough to eliminate the danger of flooding and erosion.

Two particular river-based activities were closely associated with the Thames islands, particularly those nearer to London. These were the cultivation of osier willows (*Salix viminalis*) and the trapping of eels. Historically, many of the islands were primarily used for the growing and harvesting of osier willows, which were planted to help protect the islands from erosion by the river, and were also cultivated for basket making and other crafts. Once the tree had reached a certain height, its shoots were coppiced before they became hard and unpliable. They were then woven into baskets of all shapes and sizes, which were in great demand for transporting fruit and vegetables from thriving local market gardens to the ever growing London markets. The islands were used because they were inaccessible to cattle who liked to graze on the new shoots. The willows were usually cut by itinerant willow harvesters who would transport themselves in small coracle-type boats and often built temporary shacks on the islands in which to sleep. The remnants of this industry can still be seen today on many Thames islands that are still overgrown with the progeny of crops that were harvested well into the 1930s.

Another skilled body of artisans used osier willows for more intricate work in such things as the manufacture of traps for crayfish, pottles for carrying strawberries and large basket-like structures called bucks, which were used to catch eels. Eel bucks made of osier shoots were placed upstream to catch the migrating eels. The bucks were set where there was a good current and were raised during the day to allow passage of the barges. The common eel differs from most other migratory fish in that it leaves the river to spawn. Eels breed in the Sargasso Sea at a point halfway between Bermuda and the Leeward Islands. The Thames now has a large upriver migration of elvers, which passes through the central London area in June. The mature silver eels leave the Thames during the last week in October and the first week of November. Traditionally fishermen caught eels on their way downstream in eel bucks.[4] Hence, several Thames islands were given the name 'Buck Ait'.

By the mid-nineteenth century, the extension of the railway out to places like Hampton and Shepperton enabled ordinary Londoners to enjoy a cheap day excursion to the riverside. Author Mick Sinclair explains that shooting between Teddington and Cricklade was banned in 1885 on the grounds that the river had 'come to be largely used as a place of public recreation and resort'. Railways had usurped the waterway's role as a primary transport route and, in 1897, it was ruled that passenger steamers would take precedence over barges at Richmond and Teddington locks, a reversal of previous rulings giving rights of way to cargo carriers. In the life of the Thames, it signalled a new era as a river of leisure and relaxation.[5] Thus, towards the end of the nineteenth century, the river was being used for all manner of recreational activities from angling to rowing and punting, with private houseboats often being moored alongside the Thames islands.

Languidly messing about on the river and its islands became hugely popular following the runaway success of Jerome K. Jerome's *Three Men in a Boat* (*To Say Nothing of the Dog*). After its publication in 1889, the number of registered Thames boats went up by 50 per cent and by the turn of the century, as the willow pollarding industry declined, the islands became popular for weekend and summer camping trips. Later, timber-framed chalets began to appear, firstly used just as holiday homes but eventually as permanent residences, especially by those who wanted to escape the Blitz and were fortunate enough to own a little island chalet. Today, about three quarters of the Thames islands are uninhabited. The remainder are home to small settlements, single houses or houseboats. Some

Placing eel bucks at Chiswick, 1898.

are accessed by footbridge, some by chain ferry and a few by road but most can only be reached by boat. Many of today's island dwellers are descendants of the original 'pioneer' settlers of the early part of the twentieth century. For them the pleasures of island living far outweigh the most obvious disadvantages of flooding, fire and inaccessibility.

The uninhabited islands are almost all either official or unofficial nature reserves and many are home to some rare and unique creatures. Indeed, parts of the west of Canvey Island arguably have the greatest biodiversity in Western Europe. The Thames islands are important refuges for animals and plants because being largely remote from human disturbance and grazing animals, the islands are able to support quite different and unique plant communities to the more accessible mainland banks. They are also valuable sanctuaries for wildfowl and woodland birds who take advantage of the tree cover and the absence of cats and other predators. The tranquil beauty of the islands, and their role as valuable wildlife habitats, helps preserve a rural element in the tidal Thames and provides an important corridor of wildlife habitat spanning the capital. The whole of the tidal Thames, including its islands and associated inter-tidal mud, has been identified as a Site of Metropolitan Importance due to the value placed upon its various natural habitats. The islands are also important because of their semi-natural banks. These support a waterside flora which has been considerably diminished along most of the Thames, as a result of artificial embankment.[6]

Many islands have changed their names with disconcerting regularity, some having had up to five or six names over the years. Some have intriguing or quaint names such as Lower Horse Island, Fireworks Ait, Monkey Island and the Flower Pot Islands. While they may not have the magnetic allure of coastal islands, any island dweller will argue that the Thames islands have a romantic allure of their own. Aside from their ecological importance, they are all totally individual and have indisputable aesthetic qualities. The Thames landscape is immeasurably enhanced by the presence of the islands – just imagine how impoverished the riverscape of Thameside towns such as Richmond and Maidenhead would be without their islands? Drifting in quiet isolation on the water's surface, they draw the eye and conjure up the very essence of undisturbed peace and tranquillity. In the River and Rowing Museum at Henley-on-Thames there is a delightful poster of Mole and Ratty on a summer's afternoon relaxing after their picnic on what appears to be a Thames island – possibly one of the picturesque islands around Cookham where Kenneth Graham was inspired to write *The Wind in the Willows*.

When I began this book I understood that there were only around eighty islands in the Thames. During research, however, I discovered more than double that number. I therefore decided to limit, with a few exceptions, the islands discussed to those which are completely surrounded by Thames water, rather than those that have one or more banks washed by the waters of a canal, stream or other river. As a result, I have not included the Isle of Sheppey, which is also surrounded by the rivers Medway and Swale, the Isle of Dogs and the Isle of Grain, both of which are no longer actual islands, but rather peninsulas, despite their island names remaining. Many of the lock islands are also excluded, as they were created for a specific purpose and hence do not have the random, wild irregularity that the natural islands have. Unfortunately, there are certainly a few more islands that I still haven't found but are probably lurking out there somewhere. This book, therefore, is not a definitive guide to all the Thames islands, but rather is intended as a point of reference on this fascinating topic.

I have started with the islands in the estuary, simply because this is where the larger and more interesting islands appear; we then progress upstream. As the river narrows, the islands get smaller and less interesting; in fact, there is very little to say about some islets other than to record their presence and mention their single tree. Not all Thames islands are very interesting or even picturesque; in fact some are downright creepy or unsightly. Nevertheless, whether large or small, inhabited or uninhabited, these islands are all unique: no two islands are the same. They form the skeletal backbone of the river and deserve to be recognised and recorded alongside the Thames locks, weirs and bridges.

NOTES

1   Quotation by Socialist MP John Burns, 1896
2   Wilson, D.G., *The Making of the Middle Thames* (Spurbooks Ltd: 1977) p.60
3   Dutton, S. 'Eyots and Aits', *Richmond and Twickenham Times*, 5 February 1938
4   Trimble, N. (ed.) *Life on the Thames Yesterday and Today* (Sunbury and Shepperton Local History Society: 1995) p.37
5   Sinclair, M., *The Thames – A Cultural History* (Oxford: Oxford University Press, 2007) p.xx
6   Pape, D., 'Nature Conservation in Hounslow', *London Ecology Unit Handbook 15*, 1990, p.9

1

THE ESTUARY ISLANDS

THE SHORE OF the Thames estuary is one of the least known and least explored coastal areas in Britain. Despite the unsightly urban sprawl from Basildon to Southend, there are still large stretches of undeveloped marshland on the south Essex coast. This ancient place lay remote and isolated for centuries until unregulated development engulfed it during the late nineteenth century and through the twentieth. Early maps of this area show several islands that were originally part of the mainland, but as the coastline eroded into smaller pieces, the first four islands in the Thames were formed from the silt in the river and material entering the estuary on the tides of the North Sea from the coast of East Anglia. The very first island in the estuary that is completely surrounded by Thames water is the inappropriately named **Two Tree Island** which, in fact, contains several hundred trees, albeit mostly quite small specimens.

Two Tree Island is uninhabited and lies to the north-east of Canvey Island, opposite the quaint village of Old Leigh-on-Sea. With its weatherboard cottages, cobbled streets and cockle sheds that encourage winter flocks of turnstone close inshore, Old Leigh provides a charming backdrop to the first islands on our journey up the Thames. Two Tree Island is connected to the mainland by a bridge and a small road that cuts through the island from north to south. The eastern part, with the adjoining salt marsh (170 acres) and a large area of inter-tidal mudflats (464 acres), is a nature reserve managed by the Essex Wildlife Trust (EWT). The western part belongs to Hadleigh Castle Country Park. The mudflats support dense beds of eel grass and provide a valuable feeding ground for wildfowl and waders. The concentration of thousands of these birds arriving on their autumn migration is one of Europe's most important avian migratory events.

In the eighteenth century the island was reinforced by a sea wall to protect it from the sea and make it suitable for grazing. For 150 years cattle roamed this rich salt marsh until 1910 when a sewage farm was built on its eastern tip. The island suffered further abuse in 1936 when it was bought by Southend Borough Council for use as a dumping ground for household rubbish. In 1974, having completed its waste tipping, the council granted a long lease to the Nature Conservancy Council (now English Nature), and the island was designated a national nature reserve. Within a decade it had reverted back to a natural wilderness as wildlife re-established itself in this partly man-made environment.

The salt marsh along the southern shore of the island is one of the best surviving in the Thames estuary and provides a home to grass snakes, lizards, butterflies, crickets and grasshoppers. At its western tip is a lagoon with a hide, from which you can see an extraordinary array of birdlife, including avocets, the striking coastal black and white waders with a long up-curved black beak. In recent years avocet chicks have successfully hatched on Two Tree Island. Each spring, after incidents in 2004 and 2005 when thieves stole avocet eggs just two days prior to hatching, EWT asks for volunteers to help protect the eggs. As a result, the Trust has managed to increase the breeding avocet population on Two Tree Island, with the help of hundreds of volunteers who take part in a coordinated 'egg watch' in the breeding season between 18 April and 10 June. Although most volunteers are local, some travel from as far as Durham to help protect the eggs. In 2010 nearly forty-five avocet hatchlings, as well as oystercatcher, redshank, common tern and ringed plover chicks were born on the island.

The island itself is relatively flat, consisting mainly of grassland and wild scrubland, interspersed with copses of small trees. The former rubbish tip now supports a number of interesting alien plants and garden 'escapes'. Waders such as curlew, dunlin, grey plover and knot appear in significant numbers outside the breeding season. Kestrels hover over the grassland and short-eared owls visit

11

The salt marshes on Two Tree Island, with Southend Pier in the distance.

during winter, hunting for field voles. Little paths meander across the reserve and strategically positioned benches provide wide views across the creeks, marshes and along the estuary, as well as providing a great view of Southend Pier and Hadleigh Castle, built in 1230, which overlooks the island. In many respects Two Tree Island is possibly as close as it gets to a naturalist's paradise.

Lying just off the south-western tip of Two Tree lies the infamous **Canvey Island**. This very large island covering an area of 18.45 sq. km, has a serious image problem. The name conjures up an unsavoury mix of a flat industrial landscape peppered with oil and gas storage silos and huge caravan parks. Although there is certainly a lot of light industry and some ugly silos, they are mostly confined to the south-western corner of the island and are relatively low-rise compared with those in other parts of the estuary. There are also a few tacky 1960s amusement arcades and caravan parks, but again they are relatively unobtrusive. Indeed, if the present craze for 'retro' continues, they may become an attraction themselves. Meanwhile, the islanders live in modest houses and bungalows, all neat and tidy, with the streets spotlessly clean and the people jolly and friendly. In all, despite its grim image, Canvey has a lot going for it, with a long and rich history and an amazing natural heritage.

The name Canvey is Anglo Saxon in origin, and means 'Cana's island', but manorial records of 1255 show it as 'Kaneveye'. The island is separated from the mainland to the north and west by a series of creeks in which the remains of Viking longboats have been found, as well as evidence of Danish settlement. Here the Danes are recorded to have moored their ships in the early period of their invasions. A Roman salt-making works and significant amounts of Roman pottery have also been found on Canvey.

The island, which used to be entirely marshland, is very flat, in parts lying 2m below the mean high-water level, and consequently has always been susceptible to severe flooding. In fact, it is surprising that the island has survived at all, since before sea defences were erected, the whole island was regularly flooded during the spring tides. In 1622, the owner of the marsh, Sir Henry Appleton, agreed to give about 50 acres to Joas Croppenburg, a Dutch merchant skilled in the making of dykes, if he would wall in the marsh. Thus, due to their renowned expertise in constructing

Right, from top

A Dutch cottage on Canvey Island.

The Dutch cottage on Canvey Island which is now a museum.

and repairing sea defences, in the early 1600s a colony of Dutch builders was invited to settle on Canvey under the watchful eye of the famous Dutch engineer, Sir Cornelius Vermuyden. The Dutch settlers used their formidable skills to build a series of drainage ditches across the island and enclosed 6,000 acres with a 20-mile wall around the island, which survived well into the mid-twentieth century.

As a result of this, a strong Dutch community formed on Canvey, evidence of which can still be found today in snippets of Dutch architectural detail dotted around the island and two roads that still bare Dutch names: Waarem Avenue and Vaagen Road. Two tiny early seventeenth-century octagonal cottages also remain from that time. These oddly shaped little dwellings boast many Flemish features and one of them, the 'Dutch Cottage' houses the island's museum. As well as reclaiming Canvey from its annual watery grave, the Dutch also bought religion to the island. In 1628, 200 Dutch workers petitioned the king to allow them to worship in their own language. Their request was granted and a little timber-framed chapel was built. The service and minister were to conform to the Dutch Church in London, and the Dutch elected their first pastor, Cornelius Jacobsen, who became 'Minister of the Divine Word in England in the Netherlandish community at Canvey Island.'[1] On 14 October 1704, the last Dutch minister on the island was buried at nearby Benfleet. The Dutch church was demolished in 1712, and after that the majority of the Dutch appeared to leave Canvey and the island was thereafter administered from the mainland. Two hundred years later, however, the Dutch influence was still clearly visible in 1902 when the naturalist C.J. Cornish described the general aspect of the island as 'like that part of Holland near the mouth of the "old" Rhine, but less closely cultivated and cared for'.

The windswept marshland provided rich grazing for the large numbers of sheep that traditionally roamed the marshes and sheep farming became a mainstay industry of the island until recently. For 200 years Canvey produced a uniquely flavoured sheep's cheese, the production of which was abandoned in 1720 when the strong taste of the cheese proved unpalatable. This isolated and bleak corner of Essex was a tremendously wild and inhospitable place that earned itself a reputation in the eighteenth and nineteenth centuries as a favourite haunt of riverside smuggling gangs. Like marshlands the world over Canvey was not a very healthy place to live. The inhabitants often suffered from a feverish disease called the 'ague'. According to Peter Ackroyd, in the early nineteenth century it was reported that 'only people who cared little whether they lived or died would

Right, from top

The Labworth Café, Canvey Island.

The Lobster Smack Inn, Canvey Island.

14

undertake farm work on the island'. But the ague disappeared in the middle of the nineteenth century, largely because of improved drainage and a reduced population of mosquitoes. Although this led to a gradual increase in the island population, the lack of a proper bridge meant that Canvey remained isolated and cut off from mainland amenities, and by 1880 the island still only had a population of 300.

To get a feel today of how distant and lonely a place Canvey once was, you must travel to the western part of the island to a creek called Holehaven, which Essex historian F.G. Whitnall once described as the 'World's End'. Nestling close to Holehaven and now somewhat overshadowed by the mammoth ugliness of mushrooming oil storage tanks stands the celebrated sixteenth-century Lobster Smack Inn, which is mentioned in Dickens's *Great Expectations*. A 1777 map clearly shows the quaint little weather-boarded inn as the World's End – a fitting description for this lonely pub standing at the water's edge 'twixt the city and the sea'. To visitors and inhabitants alike in the eighteenth century it must indeed have seemed like the world's end.[2]

In the latter half of the nineteenth century Canvey Village became the centre of the island. St Katherine's church was built around 1875 on the site of the original Dutch church, and today is a very attractive little whitewashed building, which has now been turned into an interesting island heritage centre. The old Red Cow pub was a small wooden building near the edge of the only road, and by 1921 the population had reached 1,795 for there was plenty of work in the island's new tourist industry. The expansion of the rail network meant that people from the overcrowded slums of East London could now enjoy a cheap day excursion to Southend and onto the sandy beaches of rural Canvey. On August bank holiday 1925, more than 50,000 Londoners flocked to Canvey, lining up six deep for an hour or more to cross to the island on one of the four ferries, or walking across a causeway of ancient stepping stones (which are preserved today outside the council offices) at low tide.

In April 1931 the long-wished-for bridge joining Canvey to the mainland was finally opened. A new road was also built across the island, as well as other modern amenities including the opening of caravan and camp sites. Canvey became a popular holiday resort enabling east Londoners to enjoy a nearby holiday with donkey rides on the sands and accommodation in makeshift chalets erected on little plots of land bought cheaply by families. As Canvey developed, its sweeping promenade began to get pretensions to grandeur with the appearance of glamorous art deco buildings. One, a casino calling itself 'Monico' in a misspelt reference to the Riviera resort, opened in 1933. This was followed in the same year by the truly striking Labworth Café, which was constructed right on the seafront. It was built by Ove Arup, the design engineer of the Sydney Opera House, in a style reminiscent of the bridge of the *Queen Mary*: it is the only building Ove Arup ever designed purely by himself.[3] It is still a welcoming café today, brazenly facing the estuary and gleaming in its sun-bleached white.

By the time the Second World War began to loom, Canvey had established itself as a popular seaside resort for Londoners, some of whom decided to up sticks and move to Canvey permanently, building the island's first brick-built bungalows. The late 1930s also saw the first of the large oil storage tanks being built on the island. This was seriously bad timing, however, because in May 1940 one of the first German air raids on England attacked the oil storage tanks near the old Lobster Smack Inn, which luckily survived unscathed. Despite this, by the close of the war, Canvey's population had risen to 10,000 as east Londoners fled the Blitz to their island holiday homes and decided to stay in them full time.

Meanwhile, in the two and a half centuries since the Dutch left Canvey, the island's sea defences had gradually deteriorated. The island had suffered extensive flooding throughout the eighteenth and nineteenth centuries when on occasion virtually the whole island was submerged, but perhaps the most devastating flood to occur was the Great Flood on the night of 31 January 1953. That night, a particularly violent storm, combined with an unusually high tide, engulfed the entire estuary; more than 300 people drowned, fifty-eight of whom were from Canvey Island. Most islanders were asleep as the water breached the defences and were not aware of the danger until the sea had reached their homes. Jonathon Schneer vividly describes that fateful night:

> The first surge, many million tons of water, and then the spring tide, many million tons more and backed by howling gales, crashed against those walls with breathtaking ferocity, overtopped them, pounded them to bits, eventually breached them and poured through. People awoke in darkness as water and debris smashed against the walls and doors and windows of their homes, forcing entrance for the icy deluge. Some made desperate by the rising water, smashed holes in their ceilings. Then they climbed through, pulling their children after them onto the rooftops.[4]

There followed a mass evacuation of the island. Canvey Village, which was built on the highest point on the island, approximately 2ft above sea level, escaped the worst effects of the flood. This area included the Red Cow pub, which was later renamed the King Canute in reference to the eleventh-century Danish king of England, who commanded the tide to halt with the sea lapping at his feet. The names of those who died that night are recorded on the island's Flood Memorial. Canvey Island's motto *Ex Mare Dei Gratia* – 'From the Sea by the Grace of God' – is apt indeed.

Under the slogan 'Canvey will rise again', the island gradually recovered. Apparently, the deluge of sea water killed so many earthworms that they subsequently had to be imported from the mainland. A new 10ft sea wall was built to protect the area from further flooding and a trickle of tourists returned. In reality, however, Canvey's day had passed. The writing was on the wall even before the floods, when in 1951 the Regent Oil Company constructed the island's largest industrial development on a 30-acre site: an oil storage installation and depot with a jetty running 800ft into the river. Despite its location at the far western corner of the island, this was to set the tone for the wider public's perception of Canvey as an industrial eyesore to be avoided. As a result, by the end of the decade the island's allure had faded and the holidaymakers began to drift away to the new continental 'package deals' in Spain and Majorca.

In November 1954 a badly decomposed carcass of an unusual creature was washed up on the shore of Canvey Island. It appears to have been a particularly grotesque specimen over 2ft in length with huge bulging eyes, reddish coloured skin and two leg-like fins. After being examined by zoologists, who were unable to name it, the carcass was incinerated. The following year yet another similar carcass found its way onto Canvey's shore but this one was nearly twice the size at 3ft 9in and weighing 25lb. It was much better preserved than the first specimen but despite a thorough examination, it remained unclear as to what species it was. Local tradition has it that both creatures were possibly anglerfish – a ferocious-looking creature that lives in the extreme depths of the ocean – but this seems unlikely given that anglerfish are on average only 5in long. The mystery remains.

Today the island's population of 37,000 lives in three settlements: Canvey Village, Newlands and Leigh Beck, all running into each other. The architecture is modern, suburban and pretty non-descript to look at. Although the sea pounds the island with every incoming tide, the islanders now have little to fear from flooding. To protect the island from the sea, yet another 15-mile-long seawall, even higher than its predecessor, was completed in 1982 and is the one we see today. The wall surrounds 75 per cent of the island's perimeter, terminating at the flood barriers spanning Benfleet Creek to the north and East Haven Creek in the west.

A new and complicated drainage system consists of sewers, culverts, natural and artificial dykes, and lakes which feed seven pumping stations and gravity sluices that discharge the water into the Thames and creeks. At first glance the sea wall appears stark and foreboding but on a bright sunny day with the glistening yellow sand below and the sheer expanse of the estuary beyond, it resembles an amazing snake-like security blanket guarding this strange but surprisingly pleasant landscape.

Just below the wall at Holehaven, the Lobster Smack Inn still retains many original features, with echoes of smugglers and long-dead sailors. Whitnall noted that up until the 1920s, crews belonging to the Dutch eel boats were commonly heard chatting in the parlour of the inn. For all the obvious changes that have taken place over the years, Holehaven retains much of its former atmosphere of calm and isolation.[5] These days, even though the completion of the new sea wall has enabled housing to be built nearby, there is still a sense of having reached the Essex version of Land's End.

The evolution of Canvey from reclaimed farmland to a makeshift holiday resort and latterly a place of industry and permanent residence has produced a marked contrast between the environments in the east and west of the island. Whereas the eastern half has evolved into a densely built-up residential area, the western part of the island is still mainly open farmland and marshes interspersed with light industrial areas. In 2010 the Royal Society for the Protection of Birds (RSPB) opened a spectacular reserve comprising 256 hectares of grazing marshes, water meadows and salt marsh on the north-west coast of the island. The marshlands in the island's south west include the Canvey Wick Nature Reserve, a designated Site of Special Scientific Interest (SSSI) that has evolved on the site of a former Occidental Oil refinery and storage complex that was built in the 1970s but never used as such. Because the foundations of the 100-hectare site were prepared by laying thousands of tonnes of silt dredged from the Thames, the abandoned and undisturbed area has flourished as a haven for around 1,300 species of wildlife, many of which are endangered or were thought to be extinct. The site is of immense national importance for the wildlife it supports, including a number of protected species such as the great crested newt, lizards, adders and water voles. In summer there are impressive displays of orchids.

Other areas of natural interest include the 8 hectares of Canvey Lake Nature Reserve. The large lake existed as a means to facilitate the salt-making process during the Roman settlement of the island, and is also thought to have been used as an oyster bed. At the eastern point of the island is the 36-acre Canvey Heights Country Park, which has been reclaimed from the Newlands landfill site that operated there between 1954 and 1989. The park supports an array of wildfowl such as skylarks, dark-bellied brent geese and grey plover. These days Canvey still attracts visitors, but apart from locals drawn to the golden sands on a sunny day, they are usually bird watchers and naturalists, for the western part of Canvey Island contains one of the highest levels of biodiversity in Western Europe.

Over the past thirty years, a new breed of tourist had been drawn to Canvey. During the 1970s, the island became a centre of the pub rock movement, featuring the original Thames Delta pub rockers Dr Feelgood and Ian Dury. Writer Christopher Somerville vividly describes how once a year, the heady days of pub rock are relived on a walk around Canvey Island, when a motley crew of music fans from all over the world meet up to honour Lee Brilleaux, the harsh-voiced singer

The sea wall, Canvey Island.

and frontman of Dr Feelgood, who died of lymphoma in 1994. Lee grew up on the island, and it was here that he formed the R&B band Dr Feelgood in the early 1970s. Somerville explains that it is to Canvey that the fans are drawn each year for the Lee Brilleaux Memorial weekend, around his birthday in early May. The Feelgood's iconic first album – *Down by the Jetty* – chronicles the moody Canvey landscape and atmosphere that shaped the band and their rough-edged music, which helped pave the way for the later punk rock explosion.[6]

There is no escaping the fact that Canvey is an extremely down-to-earth place, but scratch the surface and you find much that is unique and fascinating. The islanders, long the butt of Essex jokes, are a tough but friendly breed of 'rough diamonds' and are fiercely proud of their island, with its great sandy beaches, sweet salt breezes and magnificent flaming sunsets. From the top of the great sea wall there are amazing expansive views over the estuary far across to the shores of Kent, and then back across the west of the island with its strangely haunting windswept marshlands and their abundance of bird and wildlife. It is an exhilarating experience sitting on the old jetty watching the giant cargo ships and oil tankers glide up the glittering estuary. Although the gas and oil silos and bungaloid sprawl certainly dominate parts of Canvey, this little-regarded outcrop of Essex still manages to retain the atmosphere of an ancient place and a sense of being a very separate region.

Across Holehave Creek, between Canvey and Stanford-le-Hope, loom the flares and pipe work of a giant oil refinery that overshadows two uninhabited islands called **Lower Horse Island** and **Upper Horse Island**.

Lower Horse is the larger of the two, perhaps 4 acres in size. Both islands, which are completely flat and treeless, can clearly be seen from the old Dr Feelgood jetty on Canvey Island. From there it seems quite improbable that anything of any significance could ever have occurred on them. Yet there is evidence of Roman habitation on Upper Horse Island, with the discovery of part of a Roman fortified camp and a port. There are three small islets off Lower Horse Island that are again overshadowed by the oil refineries at Thames Haven. Nevertheless, the five areas of marshland and saltings that make up the Horse islands are teeming with wading birds and insects. The dry and relatively warm climate of this wild marsh-fringed seaboard facilitates the amazing ecological diversity of the Thames estuary.

NOTES

1   McCave, F., *A History of Canvey Island* (Ian Henry Publications: 1985) p.11

2   Whitnall, F.G., 'The World's End', *Essex Countryside*, January 1967

3   Winn, C., *I Never Knew that about the River Thames*, Ebury Press, 2010, p.236

4   Schneer, J., *The Thames, England's River* (Abacus: 2005) pp.246–7

5   Whitnall, *op. cit.*

6   Somerville, C., 'Down by the Jetty', *Coast* magazine, April 2008. For more on Dr Feelgood see www.drfeelgood.org

2

THE LONDON ISLANDS

MOVING UP INTO the industrial Thames, adjacent to Rainham Creek is the uninhabited and quite unprepossessing **Frog Island**. Approximately 4.2 hectares in area, the island is the site of the mechanical biological treatment works of the East London Waste Authority, a large waste generating plant. The old Phoenix Wharf on the island has safeguarded wharf status. Such wharves are those in London which have been given special status by the Mayor of London and the Port of London Authority to ensure that they are retained as working wharves and are protected from redevelopment for non-port purposes. In the summer of 2009 a new waste management facility was completed and opened on Frog Island. The site aims to maximise the recycling and disposal of household rubbish. The facility comprises of a mechanical biological treatment works, which processes 180,000 tonnes of rubbish which would otherwise end up in landfill. The facility turns 50 per cent of processed waste into refuse-derived fuel, and also recovers metals and glass to be re-used in industry. This island, therefore, may not be aesthetically pleasing, but the progressive work being done there is greatly reducing landfill waste for the benefit of the people of Essex.

Moving hastily on, past the stretch of the river called Gallions Reach, where on 3 September 1878 one of the greatest disasters to occur in peacetime Britain claimed the lives of more than 700 people who drowned after a pleasure steamer, the *Princess Alice*, collided with the *Bywell Castle*, a larger steamer. It could be argued that a double tragedy occurred that day because many of those who managed to swim ashore soon died from having swallowed raw sewage. An hour before the sinking, the sewage outfalls at Barking and Crossness had discharged around 75 million gallons of fermenting sewage into the Thames and into the path of the *Princess Alice*. Ten years later, one of the few survivors of this disaster, Elizabeth Stride, was to become the third victim of Jack the Ripper.

Upriver through the heart of London, past the Isle of Dogs where the Tudor monarchs of Greenwich Palace kept their hunting dogs, we come to Westminster. Of the countless Thames islands that have disappeared over time, perhaps at least one deserves a short mention and that is **Thorney Island**, which today is the area of central London known as Westminster. Once a 30-acre island lying between the Thames and two streams of the River Tyburn, it was covered with brambles and so was named Thorney ('thorn island') by the Anglo-Saxons who settled here. In the early seventh century, a small church dedicated to St Peter was built on the island, which was later given to a community of monks. It was now the church of an abbey, meaning a monastery ruled by an abbot (father) rather than a bishop (St Paul's in London was also a monastery, but it was headed by a bishop and so called a 'cathedral', from *cathedra*, the throne of a bishop). In time, the abbey came to be known as the West Minster (monastery) to distinguish it from St Paul's, the East Minster.

From Westminster we have to travel virtually the whole length of the Thames in London before coming to the next island in West London's fashionable suburb of Chiswick, **Chiswick Eyot**.

Hidden in a backwater behind the thunderous Great West Road is old Chiswick village, with its one winding road leading down to the Thames. There, opposite the ancient terrace of Chiswick Mall and its elegant Georgian and Regency houses with their beautifully manicured riverside gardens, is Chiswick Eyot.

Osier cutters on Chiswick Eyot, 1927.

*John Davidson and Tommy O'Dell cutting osiers on Chiswick Eyot in 1927. The cutters have waited
until high tide to float their load to the bank, thus avoiding carrying it across the mud.*

For those who disregard the estuary as being the river proper, it is often referred to as the first island in the Thames.

This narrow, uninhabited island, 300 metres in length, is a well-known landmark on the Boat Race course picked out by the aerial television coverage of the race, and the tall green pole just off the upstream end of the island that is used as a marker by the rowers. Others may know Chiswick Eyot from the marvellous 1953 abstract painting of the island, *The View from St Nicholas's Churchyard*, by John Trevelyan that hangs in the Tate Britain gallery.

The island covers an area of almost 4 acres, and is separated from the mainland by a narrow channel accessed by a public slipway. In fact, it stands so enticingly near to the riverbank that at low tide people often take the opportunity to walk across and explore the dense interior. Many, however, fail to notice the rapidly rising tide that rushes up the inner channel, and sometimes totally covers the island. In March 2005, seventeen people had to be rescued from the island by the Chiswick lifeboat just before it was completely covered by the high spring tide. As the lifeboat crew warn, the tide on this part of the Thames behaves differently from the coast, as it takes eight hours to ebb but only four hours to flood. This means that during the spring tides, the river level rises very rapidly covering a tidal range of up to 6 metres. Today there is a sign warning of the risk of being marooned at high tide.

Centuries ago the island was much larger than it is today, and appears to have been a place of early human settlement with flint tools and pottery dating from the Neolithic period (around 4,500–2,300 BC) being found. Roman spearheads and knives and the pommel of a Saxon sword have also been found, and at a later period the island was a camping place for Danish raiders. Over time, the area around Chiswick Eyot developed as a fishing village, before becoming a fashionable residential area during the Georgian and Regency eras. During the early summer of 1895, a porpoise was spotted just above the island, and in 1902 the last of the Chiswick fishermen was netting eels off the eyot when he caught an enormous silver eel weighing almost 4lb. During the nineteenth century, there was tremendous demand for Thames eels, which were sold at the Sunday eel market that used to be held near Blackfriars Bridge.

The Chiswick fishermen supplemented their income by harvesting osier willows. Since the mid-eighteenth century, the island had been a centre for the growing of three types of osiers – the yellow willow, the almond-leaved willow and the osier willow – and these were noted as amongst the finest on the Thames. Osier cutting took place in January, when the willow shoots were dried and stacked in bundles ready to be sold to make baskets for the nearby market gardens; fresh rods were then planted in February. The smaller osier rods were used for making crayfish pots. In spring the grass that grew among the osier stumps was sold to tradesmen with horse-drawn carts to feed their animals. During the Great Exhibition of 1851,

The osier cutter's whetstone that is now in Gunnersbury Park museum.

demand for milk was high because of the large numbers of visitors drawn to London, thus the eyot's grass fetched high prices from the keepers of stable-fed cows. The whetstone upon which the Chiswick osier cutters sharpened their knives is now displayed 2 miles away in Gunnersbury Park Museum. At one time it was placed handily at the Red Lion (now a private house with a resident ghost!) in Chiswick Mall, and at another period it was in the White Bear and Whetstone, a pub long since vanished, that stood in Chiswick Lane.[1] The cultivation of the island as a commercial osier bed continued until 1935, but regular cutting of the willows ceased after the Second World War. From then on the island began to grow wild. There used to be a ditch bisecting the island that marked the boundary between Chiswick (Middlesex) and Hammersmith (London), but this has now totally disappeared.

Looking at its recent history, it is miraculous that this little island has survived at all. Over the centuries it has suffered from severe erosion, accelerated by its position on the outside of a large northward loop of the Thames, and by the sharp increase in large and faster river traffic during the first half of the twentieth century. In fact, the island is currently only about half the size it was in the early nineteenth century. In Samuel Leigh's 1830 *Panorama of the Thames*, the island appears almost a quarter of a mile long, but by 1950 its eastern tip had completely disappeared below water, and it measured little more than the 300 metres we see today.

By the late 1950s the island was disappearing so fast that the Old Chiswick Preservation Society persuaded Brentford and Chiswick Council to try and halt erosion at the western end with balks of timber and many barge loads of shingle. This was not enough protection, however, and in 1978 Hounslow Council considered removing the entire island because debris from its eroding banks was

Oliver's Eyot, Strand-on-the-Green around 1920.

becoming a dangerous nuisance to boat-owners using the Thames. Local protests persuaded the council to preserve the island, and conservation groups and volunteers helped restore the eyot. Later, both ends of the island were reinforced with large bricks and in 1993 the London Borough of Hounslow declared the island a Local Nature Reserve. If it had not been protected from the tides, the island, like so many others in this stretch of the Thames, would almost certainly have disappeared.

Today Chiswick Eyot is a wonderful natural oasis in this highly urbanised area. It is still mostly covered by low-growing willow pollards that grow in abandoned confusion, as they have done ever since they were a main source of livelihood for Chiswick river folk. The island is still well maintained, and every two years volunteers pollard the osiers and clear any debris. It is pleasing to know that periodically some modern basket makers still come to the eyot to cut osier rods for their craft. Chiswick Eyot is unique among the Thames islands because it is the only one that is still predominantly a working osier bed. The fact that this rural activity survives here is particularly interesting given that the island is the closest one to central London. If you are prepared to squelch your way across the mud at low tide, you will be immensely rewarded by this lovely island with its little shingle beach, so perfect for a summer picnic, and the marvellous views downstream towards urban Hammersmith and upstream to leafy Kew. But do keep a wary eye on the state of the tide.

Chiswick Eyot, the inner channel.

Oliver's Eyot, 1865.

From Chiswick the river loops round to Mortlake Reach and on up past Kew Railway Bridge to **Oliver's Eyot**.

This sizeable uninhabited island, which is much higher than Chiswick Eyot, is approximately 100 metres long and 20 metres wide. It provides a striking site, positioned as it is in the very centre of the river. It used to be called Strand Eyot as it lies directly opposite the popular Strand-on-the-Green, a former Thames fishing village now fronted by very expensive and elegant Georgian and Regency houses.

The island is only accessible by boat, although providing you don't mind getting impossibly wet and muddy, it is sometimes possible to wade through the small channel of water onto the island at low tide.

The island was given its current name because Oliver Cromwell reputedly took refuge here during the Civil War. There is said to be a tunnel linking it to the nearby Bulls Head pub, and a myth has arisen that Cromwell used the pub as an intermittent headquarters. Local legend says that a woman betrayed him to Royalist forces and Cromwell escaped, probably through a tunnel, to the island in the middle of the river. Others say the tunnel was built to help Catholic priests escape from Protestant persecutors. It is not, however, improbable that Cromwell was actually in the locality, because two regiments of the Parliamentary Army were overrun by a surprise Royalist attack during the Battle of Brentford in November 1642. Nevertheless, the island was still known as Strand Eyot more than a century after the Civil War, and no evidence of a tunnel has ever been found. By the nineteenth century the story had become so woven into local mythology that Strand Eyot became Oliver's Eyot.

In 1788 the City of London purchased the island for sixty guineas to use as a base for collecting tolls from the increasing barge traffic. A large wooden structure was built on the island to house a toll collector, and a barge was moored alongside from which tolls were taken from passing boats. The toll barge had previously been stationed at Fulham Bridge before it was moved to the tail of Oliver's Eyot. For safety the island was raised 3ft and embanked at each end, giving it the height we see today. The pub directly in front of the island, The City Barge, takes its name from this toll barge. By the 1820s, however, toll collection had ceased and the island was abandoned. In September 1826 the clerk of works reported that the island was 'at present nearly useless and resorted to by persons committing nuisances and destroying the building.'[2] In 1857 the island was transferred to the Thames Conservancy Board, and by 1865 it had built a smithy to make and repair boat parts.

In 1909 Oliver's Island was again transferred from the Thames Conservancy to the Port of London Authority (PLA), which used it as a storage depot and a wharf for derelict craft. Even today, the wooden repair struts that held the boats are clearly visible, albeit in a ruined state. In 1958, local residents formed The Strand-on-the-Green Association, which took an interest in conservation on the island and was at the forefront of protests when the PLA, having no more use for the island, tried to sell it in 1971. Following strong local opposition, the plan was dropped and Oliver's Eyot was instead leased to the London Natural History Society which still manages it today.

Most of the island is covered by woodland, with several weeping willows on the south-west bank and three large Lombardy poplars in the centre of the island.

Oliver's Eyot at low tide from the Kew bank.

Shrubs include hawthorn, dogwood and cherry as well as bamboo. Efforts are being made to control non-native tree and bird species. Among the many species of typical Thames flora on the banks can be found the pink water speedwell, which is a very rare species in London. The island is a valuable nesting site and refuge for wildfowl and a wide variety of woodland birds, including woodpeckers, but the classic bird of the island is the cormorant, many of which can be seen sunning themselves on the island's banks.[3]

The centre of the island is quite eerie, being overshadowed by the dense canopy of trees and with the intermittent creaking sound of the ancient poplars. All around the ground are strewn the remains of the house which the City Corporation built for their collector when they first began levying tolls on the barge traffic in 1778, and then there are the remains of the old boatyard and the 1860s blacksmith's smithy that was demolished in 1990. Hidden in the undergrowth is a huge oblong stone plinth lying on its side with the year 1868 engraved onto it. There is also a large boundary marker, believed to be a marker between Surrey and Middlesex. In all, this is a hugely atmospheric island that due to its height and central position greatly enhances, as well as dominates, the view of the river at this point.

A downstream view of Brentford Ait.

As we pass under Kew Bridge, the Thames at Brentford gradually bends at the junction of the River Brent and the Grand Union Canal. Here we find the largest area of inter-tidal mud habitat in the upper Thames, which has an incredibly rich invertebrate fauna, including flatworms, freshwater shrimps and six species of leech. Twenty species of gastropod (mostly snails) have also been recorded and two of these – the ear snail and the trumpet ramshorn snail – have very restricted distributions. The muds are therefore a rich feeding ground for birds. Teal and Wigeon visit during the winter months, whilst other birds feed year round and nest on the islands.[4]

NOTES

1   Hailstone, C., 'Osiers and Grig Wheels, Lost Industries of the Thames', *The Thames Book*, 1974, p.9

2   Thacker, F.S., *The Thames Highway, Locks and Weirs*, vol II, 1920 (David & Charles, reprinted 1968) p.500

3   Pape, D., 'Nature Conservation in Hounslow', *London Ecology Unit Handbook 15*, 1990

4   See Thames Landscape Strategy website: www.thames-landscape-strategy.org.uk

3

THE BRENTFORD ISLANDS AND ISLEWORTH AIT

THERE ARE TWO uninhabited islands at Brentford, the large Brentford Ait and the slightly smaller Lot's Ait. At low tide, rich inter-tidal mud extends the full length of the backwater formed by these islands, both of which directly face the botanical gardens at Kew on the opposite bank of the river. Here wading birds such as snipe, dunlin and sandpiper regularly feed. Herons, kingfishers, cormorants and great- and little-crested grebes are also commonly seen around Lot's and Brentford Ait. When the tide is low, Brentford Ait actually appears to be two islands because it has a depression in the middle known as Hog Hole that is covered at high tide. This long, narrow island, which regularly floods, is only accessible by boat. It is densely covered by tall woodland – mainly crack willow, giant plane trees, poplars and alders – and is an important wildlife haven with a colony of bats and a significant heronry.

John Rocque's 1746 map shows a cluster of islands and islets in the Brentford stretch of the river that eventually consolidated into the two islands we see today. According to the influential Thames author Fred Thacker, Brentford Ait's earliest name was Makenshaw, which appeared on a tablet of 1610 in All Saints church in Fulham, the inscription of which read: 'William Payne (died in 1626) bequeathed to the poor of Fulham and Hammersmith an island called Makenshaw situated in the Thames just above Kew Bridge.' Just what the poor would have done with the island, situated some distance from Hammersmith and Fulham, remains unclear. A century later the ait was known as Steven's West. The Ealing baptism register of 1698 records the birth of Stephen, son of Steven and Anne West. The Wests had made a considerable fortune from fishing rights and owned much property locally, including the island.

In the eighteenth century, there was a notorious pub on the island called the Three Swans, which thrived on fashionable river traffic. The Swan Steps led down to the river at Brentford at the site of the crossing to this pub. In 1729 Stephen West junior was granted a publican's licence for the Swan Tavern with its fishponds and orchards. Apparently, in 1779 the island was used to facilitate romantic trysts between the king's son and his mistresses. In the memoirs of Mary ('Perdita') Robinson, the young actress recalled how before her first rendezvous with the Prince of Wales she waited at an inn on an island between Brentford and Kew until the signal of a white handkerchief being waved on the Kew shore told her that she could be rowed across the river to find the future George IV awaiting her in the moonlight.[2] At that time it seems that the pub was quite respectable and served good food. Thacker writes of a William Hickey, who, in his memoirs, speaks in 1780 of: 'having dined upon the Island off the town of Brentford, where there is a house famous for dressing pitch cocked eels and also for stewing the same fish.' Just three decades later, however, in March 1811, standards seem to have slipped when a Robert Hunter of Kew Green described the island as: 'a great nuisance to this parish and the neighbourhood on both sides of the River.' One of his reasons was that it contained a 'House of Entertainment, which has long been a harbour for men and women of the worst description, where riotous and indecent scenes are often exhibited during the summer months on Sundays.'[1]

By the early nineteenth century Brentford's riverside had become increasingly industrial and populous. Its smoking chimney stacks, warehouses and boatyards had become unsightly when viewed from across the river at Kew. To deal with this, in 1811 the island was leased to a Robert Hunter for the use of King George III for a period of twenty-one years in order that Lombardy poplars could be planted on it to shut out the view of Brentford from Kew Palace. At this time the island was still known as Steven's West, but by the 1870s it was called Twig Ait and was eventually bought outright by the Crown. The inn was almost certainly the Three Swans but no trace of it now remains.

Lot's Ait, Brentford, showing the inter-tidal mud.

Meanwhile, by the end of the nineteenth century the number of people using the river had increased dramatically. Well-to-do visitors began flocking to the new 'wonder' Kew Gardens, where they would stroll along the towpath adjacent to the beautiful new botanical gardens, trying not to be distracted by the ugliness of the opposite bank. A wonderful postcard exists, dated 16 August 1906, showing the industrial town of Brentford from the towpath on the Surrey bank. The picture depicts four well-dressed people sitting on a bench and looking across the river to the ugly smoking chimney stacks of Brentford.

Although Brentford Ait administratively is part of the Borough of Richmond, geographically, it is located on the Borough of Hounslow (formerly Brentford and Chiswick) side of the Thames, with the main channel of the river passing between the ait and the Kew towpath. Consequently, the boundary between Hounslow and Richmond actually passes between Brentford Ait and its neighbour Lot's Ait and down the centre of the backwater between Brentford Ait and the Hounslow riverbank. On 13 May 1893, the *Richmond and Twickenham Times* reported that the town council had, by planting trees on the island, 'made a praiseworthy effort to preserve the view along the borough's northern extremity, where the griminess of the Brentford Gas Works threatened to be revealed to wanderers on the Kew shore, by the gradual washing away of the two islands with their luxuriant trees.'

For years the preservation of these slowly eroding islands had been urged as a matter of importance. Although they were still owned by the Crown, Brentford Council had refused to incur the expense of maintaining the islands because they were just outside their district, and perhaps also because their town would suffer less by their loss than the other side of the river. Kew, as a small parish, could not afford the expense by itself, and it was only upon the inclusion of Kew (and with it the two islands) within the borough boundaries of Richmond that the opportunity arose to do what was required. Richmond then obtained the legal power to take the matter in hand, and the government, on behalf of the Crown, helped by accepting a low price for the islands.[3] Thus, in May 1893, as a result of shrewd business moves on the part of her advisers combined with some active lobbying by other interested parties, Queen Victoria was able to persuade the Borough of Richmond to buy the islands from her for the sum of £400.

As part of this dubious 'bargain', Richmond submitted to covenants requiring it to maintain the islands, including replanting trees where necessary, in order to preserve the islands from erosion. Having heard the news of the purchase of the islands, a grateful director of Kew Gardens, a Mr W.T. Thiselton Dyer, wrote to the mayor of Richmond to say that he was: 'delighted to see that the Corporation has purchased Twig Ait, which is so great an ornament to the river above Kew Bridge. I certainly never ventured to entertain the hope that our Corporation would confer such an immense boon upon our neighbourhood. The public at large will owe the Corporation a deep debt of gratitude.'[4] Thus, the Crown managed to successfully offload the problem of the eroding aits and the sorry saga of Richmond's island dependencies began. Half a century on, the 'boon' had turned into something of an expensive and troublesome millstone around the necks of Richmond rate payers.

The island trees had had no attention since being planted and as a result, had become a tangled, squalid mess. A detailed account of how badly dilapidated the islands had become appeared in a report by Richmond Parks Committee on 10 March 1949, which read: 'Although the downstream end of the island has had protective work carried out just prior to the recent war, the remainder of the camp-shedding is in very poor condition. Several serious collapses have taken place and others are imminent. Erosion is also undermining the trees and it is now necessary to maintain lighted wreck signs, involving regular inspections and action.' In fact, overhanging branches on the Brentford Aits had become such a serious danger to passing river traffic that the Port of London Authority (PLA) issued a warning that they might be forced to take legal action to compel the council to maintain the islands.

On 12 October 1956, Richmond Council reported that:

> The Council is fully aware of its responsibilities towards these 'gifts' from Queen Victoria, which are proving a costly burden for the ratepayers. It is a long and sad story, and little did the predecessors of the present council think their action would lead to such a financial liability being imposed upon the inhabitants of Richmond. They did not foresee the development of engine-driven barges, the stream of tugs and pleasure steamers, cabin cruisers and motor boats, which are mainly responsible for the damage done by the constant wash.

As a result of the PLA's report, on 6 October fifteen members of Richmond Council toured the islands on a launch to inspect the erosion on all the Thames islands between Kew Bridge and Teddington Lock. The cost of restoring their bank defences alone was subsequently estimated at £50,000: a considerable sum in 1956.

There now began a battle to see who would pay. The PLA had been particularly alarmed at the state of the decaying camp-shedding around the islands, but did not put forward any scheme for repairing the aits themselves. Instead they suggested that Richmond Council should approach the North Thames Gas Board (NTGB), given that the board appeared to be the only body which at that time derived any commercial benefit from the islands. By an agreement dated 21 October 1930, the Gas, Light and Coke Company had been granted permission to place water pipes, connected to the adjacent gas works on the islands, in return for a payment of a shilling a year: a sum which in 1956 was still being paid by its successor, the NTGB.

The downstream end of Lot's Ait, Brentford.

Because of the condition of the aits, Richmond Council told the NTGB that it was thinking of terminating its agreement with them.

While the wrangling persisted, the islands continued to deteriorate, so much so that navigation around them was becoming extremely hazardous due to falling trees and protruding obstructions. Eventually, after much hand-wringing, NTGB, Surrey County Council and the PLA agreed to bear part of the cost; as a result the rate payers of Richmond had to find only £36,000 of the £50,000 estimate for restoring the defences.

In March 1960 work began on restoring the islands to a decent condition, after so many years of neglect. Richmond Council planted 120 forest trees and 500 smaller trees on Brentford Ait to shield the view of Brentford Gas Works from the Richmond bank. Further tree planting occurred between 1962 and 1964.

As with its five other island dependencies, Richmond Council is still obliged to maintain the Brentford islands, despite having been jollied into buying them purely so that the view from Kew Gardens could be preserved. These days, Brentford Ait, with its (now huge) trees planted all those years ago, certainly serves its purpose in providing a pleasant view from the Kew bank. Nevertheless, it is worth reflecting that if it wasn't for the importance of Kew Gardens, these beautiful islands would almost certainly have been allowed to gradually erode and eventually disappear entirely.

Just a few yards upstream of Brentford Ait lies **Lot's Ait.** This relatively large island of around 51,000 sq. ft lies at the tip of Brentford Ait, and was once known as Barbel Island after the Barbel fish commonly found in this stretch of the Thames. Lying tucked into the back channel of Brentford Ait, Lot's has been shielded from much of the damage usually caused by the wash from river traffic. The island can only be accessed by boat because the quick-sinking mud can be highly dangerous if crossed on foot. A tithe map of 1839 shows Lot's Ait as an osier ground with willows planted along the edge of the island in order to help bind the banks. While willows still dominate the northern part of the island, the southern end is commanded by two tall Lombardy poplars and a black poplar. Purple loosestrife is common here and provides a delightful splash of colour.[5]

The natural part of the island then is quite appealing. In the centre of the ait, however, facing Brentford, sits a huge derelict boat maintenance dock, while at the upstream end, skulking in the mud, lies the rotting hulk of an old barge. In the 1920s a boatyard was established on Lot's Ait where commercial boats were built and reparied until the introduction of containerisation in the 1960s brought about a decline in commercial river traffic. The boatyard has been abandoned since 1980 and since then there have been endless planning applications put forward to develop the island. In 2002 the whole island was offered for sale with outline planning permission for a restaurant, a leisure facility and boat storage.

Unlike Brentford Ait, Richmond Council does not own all of this island but only the 45ft-wide strip that runs the length of the island on the side facing Kew Gardens. The history of the transaction whereby Richmond came into possession of this strip of land is as follows. In 1926, the island was owned by the Thames Steam Tug and Lighterage Company Ltd. The Port of London Authority gave the company permission to construct three barge repairing docks on the island but Brentford Council refused to give their consent. The company appealed, and a local inquiry was held, with the result that the major part of the island was classified as an industrial zone, while the remainder of the island (the 45ft strip previously mentioned) was zoned as land not to be built over. The barge repair docks were subsequently built.

Under this directive it was agreed that the company would plant the strip of land with trees and convey it to either Brentford Council or Richmond Borough Council to be held in perpetuity by that council as an open space without any right of public access. Apparently Brentford didn't want the land, as its council drew up a conveyance on 24 June 1929 that gave the strip of land to Richmond Council outright, without any compensation. Thus Richmond acquired yet another dubious and financially draining 'gift' because the conveyance required that Richmond

Council must 'at all times maintain the strip of land by such camp shedding as may be necessary and to maintain and replace trees if necessary.'

Lot's Ait's main claim to fame came in 1951 when the island was the unlikely setting for several scenes in the film *The African Queen*, starring Humphrey Bogart and Katharine Hepburn. The film, which was set in German East Africa during the First World War, was made by the now defunct Isleworth Studios and won Bogart his only Oscar. Although the film was also shot on location in Africa, most of the river scenes were filmed at Lot's Ait. With its dense foliage and channel between the much larger Brentford Ait, the island, with a great leap of imagination, could be portrayed as a tropical African river. In the opening scenes, when Charlie is teaching Miss Rosie to steer the *African Queen*, the backdrop of weeping willows clearly identifies this as a Thames-side bank. Throughout the film the Thames is livened up by the sound of tropical birdsong and the occasional sight of a palm (probably borrowed from neighbouring Kew Gardens) nestling among the osier willows.

After the Thames Tug and Lighterage Company's barge-building and repair works closed in 1980, Lot's Ait quickly reverted to a natural wilderness and wildlife haven. Today the old boatyard is slowly being devoured by nature and the island as a whole is now in a sorry state of eerie abandonment. The future for Lot's Ait looks very encouraging, however, as the historic boatyard is to be restored by John's Boat Works Ltd. Here small commercial vessels as well as traditional boats will be repaired and stored when the boatyard re-opens in spring 2012. The strip of land fronting the island's outer channel, which is still owned by Richmond Borough, is to remain in its natural state as a habitat for wildlife and a screen to protect the view from Kew Gardens.

From Lot's Ait the river winds through the majestic sweep of Syon Reach, providing one of the finest views on the Thames, with the gardens of Kew on the left and the last truly natural piece of London's riverbank at Syon Park on the right. Then, across from old Isleworth Village is the splendid **Isleworth Ait.**

This very large, long uninhabited island lies directly opposite the famous London Apprentice pub in old Isleworth. Although it is separated from the Middlesex bank by just a narrow channel, the ait is only accessible by boat as, like the Brentford Islands, the quick-sinking mud makes it very dangerous to try to cross the channel at low tide. What is most striking about this impressive island is the enormous height of the trees that form a dense and extensive canopy of mixed woodland. These are mainly osier willow, swamp cyprus and black poplar trees, plus a rare dawn redwood, probably an escapee from nearby Kew Gardens. The dense woodland provides a unique wildlife sanctuary because it is so rarely visited by

Isleworth Ait, Isleworth.

anyone other than volunteers from the Hounslow branch of the London Wildlife Trust. The charity leases the site from Thames Water and manages the island as a wildlife reserve. The island was previously owned by the Duke of Northumberland, who sold it to the Metropolitan Water Board in the 1930s. At that time, the island was known as Walnut Tree Ait.

The island has an area of 10 acres, parts of which flood regularly. It has a rich variety of flora and fauna providing a unique London habitat for more than fifty species of wildlife, including kingfishers, woodpeckers, tree-creepers, herons, parakeets and three rare species of beetles. Great crested grebes regularly breed here, and in all, fifty-seven species of birds have been recorded visiting the island. Isleworth Ait's most famous residents, however, are two extremely rare species of molluscs: the little two-lipped door snail (*Laciniaria biplicata*) and the even smaller German hairy snail (*Perforatella rubiginosa*). The former, with its long, elegant shell, lives almost exclusively along the Thames in London with the exception of one colony in Purfleet in Essex. The German hairy snail is also found along the Thames in London, Oxfordshire, and in small pockets along the River Medway in Kent. The latter is thought to grow hairs through its shell to allow the mollusc to sweat off moisture so that the slime it produces becomes stickier, allowing the

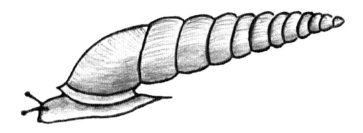

The Two-lipped Door Snail found on Isleworth Ait.

The German Hairy Snail found on Isleworth Ait.

creature to better adhere to the plants it feeds on. Both snails thrive on the island. This wealth of wildlife has led to Isleworth Ait's designation as a Local Nature Reserve with the support of Natural England.

The evolution of Isleworth Ait shows the highly transient nature of the Thames islands. Confusingly, throughout its long history the ait has changed size and shape numerous times. Maps dated 1635 show four separate islands, but by 1746 John Rocque's map shows the aits had merged to become two islands. By 1786 it had morphed back into three islands, remaining as such until the 1920s when it became a single island. The Ordnance Survey map of 1865 shows a pool on the island which it is believed was used for swimming by local schools, although there is no trace of it now. This map also shows the ait divided into two by a channel about half way along its length. Until the mid-1930s the ait was regularly flooded, but the arrival in 1935 of the Mogden sewage works caused the island to be raised by a metre, thus creating a more permanent habitat for ground nesting creatures. In 1936, the channel separating the two parts of the island was filled in.

The side of the island facing Richmond has been reinforced with vertical steel-piled banks, while the bank facing Isleworth village is natural, though much of it is taken up by a boatyard and moored boats. There is a clearly marked path which runs the entire length of the island, and in parts the canopy of trees is so dense that it becomes dark and somewhat creepy. On the northern shore the tree cover gives way and the light streams onto osier beds, which is a welcoming sight. The island was once a centre for the production of the osier willow, which was harvested by local basket makers. There are a couple of boat maintenance yards on the western side of the island, along with some houseboats moored below them and there is a small mooring and landing stage at the south-western tip. A sloping walkway leads onto a bridge and into a clearing where a map of the island explains a little of its history and depicts drawings of the ait's precious snail inhabitants.

Isleworth Ait provides a peaceful sanctuary for such a large variety of wildlife that it has become one of London Wildlife Trust's most important and unusual reserves. It can only be visited by previous arrangement with the Trust, who organise monthly volunteer work parties to harvest osiers. These are then used for weaving demonstrations provided for visitors and parties of London schoolchildren. To learn more about this remarkable island or to take part in regular work parties contact the trust.

NOTES

1   Thacker, F.S., *The Thames Highway*, Vol.II, 1920 (Newton Abbot: David & Charles, reprinted 1968) pp.492–3

2   *The Times*, 10 October 1956

3   *Richmond and Twickenham Times*, 13 May 1893

4   *Thames Valley Times*, 10 May 1893

5   See 'Nature Conservation in Hounslow', *London Ecology Unit Handbook 15*, 1990

4

THE RICHMOND ISLANDS

THE NEXT GROUP of islands are situated in the impressive and historic town of Richmond. Along with Lot's Ait and Brentford Ait, the four islands in this group are collectively known as Richmond's Island Dependencies. As we pass under Richmond Railway Bridge, like two sentries guarding the river's entrance to the town, are the charming little **Flower Pot Islands.**

These two minute, almost circular mounds, with their mass of foliage flopping over the edge of their stone camp-shedding, were once one fair-sized island almost equal in size to the neighbouring Corporation Island. Apparently, for some unknown reason, the Duke of Queensbury had the downstream island cut in two around 1776, and subsequent tidal erosion then reduced it to the two tiny eyots we see today. Until the late 1950s they were known as the Two Tree Islands. The second of these (nearest to Richmond Bridge) is the more attractive with a greater number of trees. The first islet has fewer trees – just a solitary maple and three small willows. Herons nest on both islands.

Twenty years before buying Brentford Ait, Richmond Council purchased the Flower Pot Islands from Queen Victoria for £200 in 1873. The royal covenant was subject to the following conditions: '(a) the islands to be used for ever by the inhabitants and parishioners of the parish of Richmond and others as a pleasure ground; (b) at all times thereafter to maintain and to keep in good repair and condition, and at all times preserve and maintain the ornamental character of the islands and the trees growing thereon and also the banks from destruction and decay.' Until the end of the nineteenth century, Richmond Council observed the covenant's conditions and the islets were pretty well maintained. For the first half of the twentieth century, however, the islands suffered from severe neglect. In June 1948 the Port of London Authority reported that the condition of the islands was becoming very dangerous, but the cost of removing them altogether would be greater than the cost of repair. In March 1949, the borough engineer and surveyor Mr Stanley Weddle, reported on the condition of the Flower Pot Islands, saying: 'These two small eyots are at present supported by light timber camp-shedding looped with steel, but both islands are in urgent need of stronger protective works if they are going to be saved.'

The fact that these two islets exist at all is a miracle, as they appeared completely doomed in October 1956 when the *Richmond Herald* reported that 'the felling of a major tree on one of the small tree islands was no doubt necessary for safety as it was in very poor health. No one can doubt that the danger from the trees springs from the appalling condition of the retaining walls to these islands. Indeed, they now hardly exist as the earth is being washed out from amongst the roots, leaving insufficient weight to ensure stability.' The following month the fate of the little aits appeared sealed when the borough's Parks Committee submitted another report on the condition of Richmond's seven islands (Brentford Ait was classified as two islands) in which it was recommended that the two islets 'be allowed to eventually erode away after the trees on them had been rendered safe'.

Thankfully there was a reprieve. Two years on from deciding that the Flower Pot Islands should be allowed to disappear, Richmond Council was able to rescind the decision after Surrey County Council offered, in September 1958, to pay 50 per cent of the cost of repairing the camp-shedding, not only on the two Flower Pot Islands, but on Richmond's other islands as well. The little aits were spared, and today they are a charming feature of the river at Richmond. It must be remembered, however, that beauty has its cost. It is to be hoped then that the present Richmond Council does not neglect these islands to the shameful extent of its predecessors.

The second Flower Pot Island, Richmond.

Corporation Island, Richmond.

Glover's Island, Richmond.

Just a few yards along, almost in the shadow of Richmond Bridge, lies **Corporation Island.** This long, narrow, uninhabited island is situated directly opposite Richmond's impressive river frontage, which was designed in the 1980s by architect Quinlan Terry. The island, which often gets washed over at high tide, is home to herons, coots, moorhens and several colonies of ducks and geese that nest in the sparsely wooded interior. On the northern shore a number of old, rotting boats lie covered in foliage interspersed with a few newer craft, otherwise the island is completely undisturbed. In summer it exudes an eerie quiet and calm, in marked contrast to the adjacent grand promenade where the world and his mother throng.

Corporation Island has a long history going back to at least 1602, when it was owned by John Standen and was then known as the Bullrush Bed. It was purchased by the Duke of Queensbury in 1802. Both the Flowerpot Islands and the Bullrush Bed were sold to the Richmond Vestry for £200 by the commissioners of woods in 1873. The Bullrush Bed was then renamed Corporation Island to commemorate Richmond becoming a borough in 1890.

A newspaper photograph taken in February 1907 shows the 'picturesque' Corporation Island as lying much lower than it does today, with virtually no protection to its banks, but with disproportionately large trees upon it. One can only presume that it was the roots of the trees that prevented the island from eroding. Over the next fifty years the island's trees and shrubs grew to a point where they represented a danger to navigation. Thus, in March 1960, the council ordered their removal, much to the dismay of local residents. The *Richmond Herald* reported that:

Once a mass of greenery, Corporation Island today presents a desolate site. The huge trees which for more than a century graced Corporation Island are no more. Just two small trees are left clinging desperately to the very rim of the island, a pathetic sight indeed. The island is now bare, to await a new population of smaller trees which are more suitable for the wet location. The trees left their island home unceremoniously hacked into huge chunks and towed away on barges. Thus, Richmond Council reduced Corporation Island to a mud bank by the simple process of destroying every vestige of tree and plant life on it.

A month later the local press reported on the:

Rebirth of an Island. Tree planting is in progress on Corporation Island. Two kinds of trees are to replace the ill-rooted forest of green which was lumbered so brutally just a month before. Four year old weeping willows, 16ft in height, were planted around the island's perimeter, and Swamp Cypress of the same age but only 3ft in height were planted in the centre of the island.

In all sixty trees were planted, and fifty years on the trees we see today are almost fully matured and fulfil their purpose of stabilising erosion, providing a home for wildlife and forming a picturesque feature of Richmond's riverscape.

Above Richmond Bridge, as the river rounds Horse Reach bend, we come to the imposing **Glover's Island.**

This fair-sized, uninhabited island lies directly opposite Petersham Meadows, and was originally known as Petersham Ait. Of all of Richmond's islands, Glover's has to be the jewel in the crown. From a purely visual aspect this must surely be the most famous of all Thames islands, as it forms the centrepiece of the spectacular view from Richmond Hill, one of the most protected views in Britain. Indeed, the view from Richmond Hill is the first and only view in England to be protected by an Act of Parliament – the Richmond, Ham and Petersham Open Spaces Act of 1902.[1]

It is a very impressive island, raised to its present height by rubble from the excavation of the London tube network being dumped on it during the middle of the nineteenth century. The island is so well protected by concrete camp-shedding that it is virtually impossible to land upon. It is very heavily wooded with an almost impenetrable interior. There are four giant plane trees and several clumps of bamboo interspersed with tangled shrubs and the remnants of old fruit trees.

Like many Thames islands, Glover's seems to have changed shape over the years. Early photos taken around the turn of the twentieth century show the island to be much wider than it is today; a century before, however, it appears much smaller and thinner. A large Turner painting of Richmond Hill in 1819 depicts the famous view from the hill over Petersham Meadow, in which Glover's Island appears as a very thin strip of grassland or perhaps of coppiced willows with no trees at all. At that time the island had not been raised or protected by camp-shedding and presumably would have been flooded at high tide.

It is highly probable that 200 years ago Glover's Island had a twin. Local historian Sydney Dutton mentions a coloured print by Grignion's called 'A View from Richmond Hill up the River', after Heckel (1749), that depicts two narrow islands opposite Marble Hill. One of the aits was long and tapering, and the river at this point divided into three channels; the two islands were side by side with a narrow channel between them. In 1794 Sir John Rennie referred to these two islands as 'The Routs': the larger island was identified as Glover's Island. Around the middle of the nineteenth century, the smaller island had in all probability been washed away after its centre had been utilised in the strengthening of the larger ait.[2]

The island owes its present name to a local boatman, J. Glover of Richmond, who in January 1872 bought the island for £70 and was permitted to enclose it with stakes for protection against erosion. On it he built a boathouse, a large workshop and a dry dock as well as a garden with fruit trees. We can still see the descendents of these today, as well as some debris from the old boatyard and workshop lying buried under foliage. Twenty years later Mr Glover tried to sell the island at auction but it failed to sell. In order to encourage the genteel folk of Richmond into forcing their council to buy the island, he suggested that he might sell it to Pears Soap Company, who could then erect a giant advertising hoarding on it. The asking price was £4,000, but Richmond Council could not justify paying this from its limited funds simply to protect the view. Glover tried again in 1898, attempting to sell the island at auction, but withdrew it when the highest bid received was only £200. Eventually, in 1900, a wealthy local resident, Max Waechter, who lived in Terrace House, Richmond Hill, bought the island for an undisclosed amount and gave it to the council. And so another of Richmond's islands was saved from a sad fate, but on a less positive note Richmond acquired yet another financially draining island dependency.

By 1952 Richmond council had had enough of being a colonial power. Such was the concern about the cost of repairing Richmond's islands that it was suggested by some that the council should give them all back to the Royal family. On 22 March 1952 the *Richmond and Twickenham Times* reported that: 'The seven Thames islands are too costly for Richmond Council which cannot afford to maintain them. The Council's Parks Committee has asked the Commissioners of Crown Lands to be released from covenants relating to the seven islands – the two Brentford Aits, Lot's Ait, Corporation Island, the Two Tree Islands, and Glover's Island.' Their request went unheeded but the debate raged on in ever more illustrious circles.

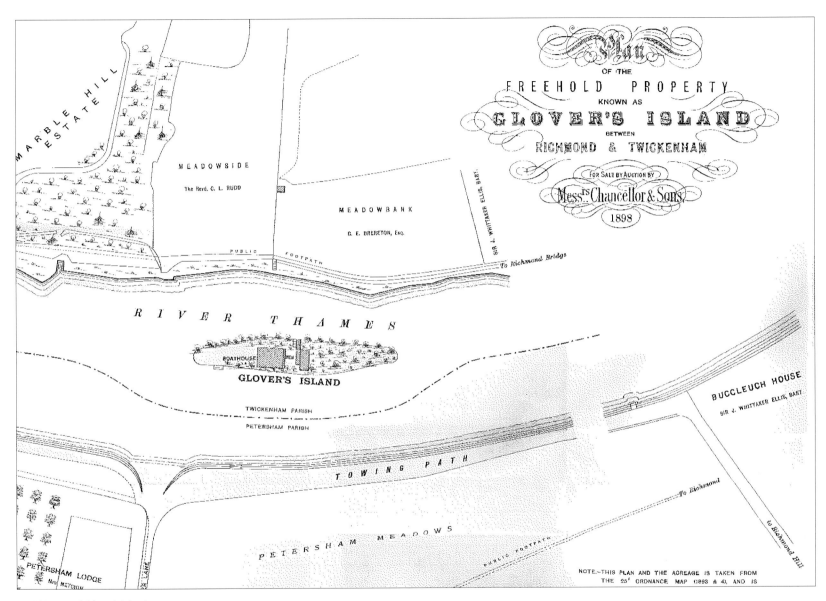

A 1898 map of Glover's Island.

On 8 October 1956, even *The Times* ran an editorial called 'The Reluctant Imperialists of Richmond – Council's Trouble with its Island Dependencies':

Among the more reluctant Imperial powers of today is Richmond Borough Council. Unknown to many of its citizens, it possesses half a dozen island dependencies along the Thames. According to Mr F. Gains, Chairman of the council parks committee, these were presented to the authority some 50 or 60 years ago by Queen Victoria, a woman with a fine sense of what should be neither seen nor heard, so that the view from the Richmond bank could be preserved permanently from the rude, unpleasing world of gas works, timber merchant and steam laundry which had started up on the other side of the river. With that agreement went the stipulation that they should be kept in good order. That is where the reluctance comes in. In 1949 the cost of repairing the camp-shedding around the islands was estimated to be about £32,000. As a result the council has put off the hour of decision, only to be threatened with legal action by the Port of London Authority if they do not maintain the islands. No wonder that in these circumstances Richmond is no longer so grateful for their Victorian legacy or that Mr. Gaines should cry bitterly of the islands: 'Anyone who wants them can have them tomorrow, free of charge.' On this empire he would gladly see the sun set.

A suggestion that the Prince of Wales should be presented with one of Richmond's islands was made by the Mayor of Croydon, Alderman. J. Kendall, in a speech of welcome to Labour members of Richmond Council on 15 August 1958. The Mayor of Richmond, Councillor J. Harwood, replied, saying that he liked the suggestion: 'In fact, I feel quite confident the Council would pass a unanimous vote that he could have the whole string.'[3] Thankfully, over the next few decades, Richmond became a wealthier borough, so the aesthetic value of the islands could take precedence over the financial cost of maintaining them. The whole character of this reach of the river particularly depends on this repartition of islands. The people of Richmond today possibly take their islands for granted but surely none would think of returning them to the Crown.

Leaving Glover's Island upstream past the grounds of Marble Hill Park and Ham House, at the site of the present White Swan pub on Twickenham's riverbank, there was once a small island called Swan Ait. In Cooke's handbook for Richmond and Twickenham, published in 1842, there is a small engraving of Swan Ait, which faced the grounds of Orleans House. Lord Kilmorey, during his time there in about 1846, was allowed to join the ait to his grounds via a solid causeway, despite much local protest. The site of the ait is now incorporated into Orleans Gardens, once the grounds of Orleans House. Just a few yards upstream from here looms the most famous island on the Thames – the legendry **Eel Pie Island**.

NOTES

1   Winn, C., *I Never Knew That about the River Thames* (Ebury Press: 2010) p.160
2   Dutton, S., 'Footnotes to Local History', *Richmond and Twickenham Times*, 5 February 1938
3   The *Richmond Herald*, 14 August 1958, p.3

5

EEL PIE ISLAND

BY FAR THE most famous island in the Thames, Eel Pie is the first inhabited island since leaving the estuary and Canvey Island. It has an almost mythical status among Londoners of a certain age who remember the birth of the R&B music scene in the early 1960s. Even without its extraordinary musical legacy, the island is an imposing spectacle to behold. It is very large: around 5 acres and approximately a third of a mile long. It commands a central position in the river with some huge trees crowning two designated wildlife areas at each end of the island, planted to preserve the stunning views from upstream and downstream. There are no cars on the island, which is reached by a gracefully arched footbridge that connects it to the mainland from the Twickenham bank. These days, with a residential population of 120 living on the island itself, and a collection of houseboats on the northern bank, it is a very tranquil place, but this hasn't always been the case.

The island was once connected to the Twickenham bank by a prehistoric causeway, and very early maps show it as three separate islets, while Rocque's 1741 map shows it in two parts. There is evidence of ancient human settlement with Mesolithic and Neolithic artefacts such as flints, horn implements, axes and hammers having been found on the island and the surrounding river bed. The island's evocative name is a tribute to the famous eel pies that were served here in the sixteenth century. Henry VIII was said to be partial to them, although no records have been found to substantiate this. Previously the island had been known as Twickenham Ait, then Parish Ait when it belonged to the local church, and later Osier Ait when it was mainly planted with osier willows for basket making. In the early 1740s a small inn called The Ship in the Ayte was built on the island, which was later renamed The White Cross. From a small shed, separate from the inn, were sold the famous eel pies that in due course led to the renaming of the island.

The White Cross was eventually demolished in 1830 and replaced by a much larger establishment called the Eel Pie Hotel, which became a popular destination for vacationing Londoners and became quite notorious in the island's later history. In *Nicholas Nickleby* (1839) Charles Dickens related that 'Miss Morleena Kenwigs had received an invitation to repair next day, per steamer from Westminster Bridge, unto the Eel Pie Island at Twickenham: there to make merry upon a cold collation, bottled beer, shrub and shrimps and to dance in the open air to the music of a locomotive band conveyed thither for the purpose…' Victorian traveller John Fisher Murray, in his 'Environs of London' of 1842 writes: 'Upon this ait a House of Entertainment has been erected, and here the river steamers land great numbers of holiday folks desirous of the delights of pure air and solicitous to banquet upon eel-pies for which the tavern is famed.' It is during this period that Eel Pie Island earned the rather derogatory description: 'fifty drunks clinging to a mud flat'.

As the popularity of the island grew, increasingly large boats tried to reach it. In order to accommodate them, in 1862 the northern channel was dredged to give an additional depth of 4ft. For the remainder of the nineteenth century Eel Pie was still predominantly used for osier cultivation. A map of 1873 shows the central part of the island as an osier ground with a large kitchen garden on the Twickenham side, and the hotel's bowling green on the Ham side. By 1892, however, the island had become partially developed with a joiner's and several boat builder's sheds, stores and engine houses having been built over the former kitchen garden. The following year the Thames Electric & Steam Launch Works cut a dock running from the main channel to the backwater leaving just a small strip of land of theirs on the end of the island. In the 1890s the hotel was the only riverside hotel between Putney and Twickenham, and on August Bank Holiday 1898, more than 10,000 people were on the island.[1]

Early morning at Eel Pie Island, showing the downstream nature reserve.

Eel Pie's popularity continued, and the first little wooden weekend chalets began to appear on the northern bank of the island, allegedly built, like those on many other Thames islands, to house the mistresses of local businessmen. During the 1920s until the outbreak of the Second World War, the hotel hosted popular tea dances but it was the last owner of the Eel Pie Island Hotel, a local antiques dealer called Michael Snapper (1908–2006), who really put Eel Pie on the map. Having acquired the hotel in 1951, he registered a company called Eel Pie Entertainments, and under his and his colleague Arthur Chisnall's direction the infamous and colourful rock and roll history of Eel Pie Island began.

By the spring of 1952 young jazz and skiffle fans were flocking to the island for concerts that were initially free of charge. As Arthur Chisnall described, there were 'hundreds of art students, beatniks, jazz buffs and plain old pleasure seekers, who, having discovered Eel Pie Island, never really went away for the next eleven years.'[2] Eventually, following a request from the local police, in August 1956 Chisnall set up a more formal club, the Eelpiland Jazz Club, with its unique membership cards in the form of little passports bearing the title 'Passport to Eelpiland'. Performers in those early days included Lonnie Donegan, Acker Bilk, Alexis Corner and Cyril Davies. Until the first footbridge was built in 1957, access to the island was via a chain barge. George Melly, who performed regularly on the island, described its otherworldliness. 'In those days you couldn't get to it by bridge. You had to get in a punt and an old man like Charon would haul you across on a chain. It was a wonderfully decaying place: there was the hotel and collapsing sheds and overgrown shrubbery.'[3] Later, in the early 1960s, one former Eelpiland regular recalls that 'Charon' was replaced by 'an old crone with a beehive hairdo who charged 2d'.

So many celebrated musical careers began on this remarkable island. Just about everyone who was a name in the world of jazz, R&B and early rock in the 1950s, '60s and early '70s played on Eel Pie. Here, Ian McLagan, later pianist for the Small Faces and the Faces first met Rod Stewart, who was playing at the time with Long John Baldry, who in turn admits that his career began on Eel Pie, as did Rod Stewart's after Baldry came across Stewart playing harmonica at Twickenham Station, and asked him if he wanted to join his band. Jeff Beck played there with his first group, the Tridents.

Dan Van Der Vat and Michele Whitby tell us that in 1963 The Rolling Stones played fourteen gigs on the island to huge crowds that stretched long over the bridge. Under the title of Davie Jones and the Manish Boys, a seventeen year old performed half a dozen times in 1964, playing support to Long John Baldry and Alex Harvey. He went on to change his name and become the superstar David Bowie.[4] Other legendary personalities and bands that played on the island included the Yardbirds, John Mayall's Bluesbreakers and Eric Clapton, Jimmy Page, John Lee

The Eel Pie Island Hotel, 1905.

Hooker, Jimmy Cliff, Pink Floyd and Fairport Convention. Eel Pie's rock and roll days were immortalised in George Harrison's 'Cockamanie Business':

> Bust my back on the Levy,
> Broke my strings on the BBC,
> Found my chops on Eel Pie Island,
> Paid my dues at the Marquee.

Meanwhile, despite Eelpiland's incredible popularity among the youth, many of the older generation were shocked by the decadence and 'outrageous' behaviour of the young revellers. They saw the island as a crime-ridden den of vice that was corrupting young people by encouraging the use of drugs, underage drinking and sexual promiscuity. They were not far wrong, as there was an abundance of cheap cider and cannabis and George Melly reckoned you could see 'sex rising from it like steam from a kettle'.[5] It was therefore only a matter of time before the establishment made its move to close down Eelpiland. The decrepit old hotel was dangerously falling apart and the police threatened it with closure. Facing an impossibly high repair bill, the hotel was forced to close its doors on 4 September 1967 for failing to comply with licensing and safety regulations.

Although Snapper reopened the Eel Pie Hotel in May the following year, it never quite matched the hedonistic devil-may-care spirit of Eelpiland, but it still attracted some famous bands such as The Who, Black Sabbath, Deep Purple, Atomic Rooster, The Edgar Broughton Band, Hawkwind and Rory Gallagher. During the 1980s, Pete Townshend was so taken with the island that he named his publishing company, Eel Pie Publishing Limited. Nevertheless, the rot had set in and by the late summer of 1969 an assortment of squatters, anarchists and commune members from around

The upstream nature reserve on Eel Pie Island.

The bridge access to Eel Pie Island.

Eel Pie Island from the Twickenham bank.

the country flocked to the Eel Pie Hotel, which became their doss house. During the winter of 1970–1 the gas and electricity were cut off, so the inhabitants began to cannibalise the very structure of their home by ripping timber from the floors, walls and stairs to burn for warmth.[6] The council eventually declared the hotel unfit for human habitation and a demolition order was served. On 2 March 1971 Michael Snapper submitted a planning application for a housing development on the hotel site. Then, less than a month later, on the morning of 30 March, a mysterious fire broke out at the hotel, leaving it partially destroyed. This conveniently paved the way for the total demolition of the old hotel, which had stood on the island for 141 years. It was replaced by a small development of townhouses called Aquarius, and thus began the gradual gentrification of Eel Pie Island that has continued to the present day.

In the two decades following the demolition of the hotel, island life continued at a leisurely pace. Although by now largely residential, Eel Pie also sustained a small boat maintenance yard and creative community, with artists and craftspeople working alongside the boatyard in the chaotic array of ramshackle buildings that made up the Marine Centre at the western end of the island. Then disaster struck. In the early hours of 3 November 1996, a terrible fire engulfed most of the Marine Centre's workshops, destroying virtually everything and causing £2 million worth of damage. Although nobody was killed or injured it was a devastating blow to the sixty uninsured artists and craftspeople, many of whom lost their entire livelihoods. No insurer would have contemplated insuring the chaotic little warren of studios that had made up Eel Pie's 'industrial' quarter. Other island residents, together with mainlanders living directly opposite the island, quickly raised more than £40,000 to help some of the victims restart their businesses, but others never recovered. In a further blow the following year the footbridge was severely damaged by a utilities contractor, so much so that it was closed by the council and the islanders were forced to use a punt to haul themselves across the river until a new bridge was opened in August 1998. These incidents only served to demonstrate that sometimes island life can be anything but idyllic.

Nevertheless, anyone crossing the bridge today can sense an immediate detachment from the hustle and bustle of Twickenham. Down the centre of the island runs a little lane flanked by thick hedges camouflaging the entrances to Eel Pie's fifty or so homes. These range from pretty little weatherboard cottages to stylish new architect-designed houses. On the south side of the island there is an eclectic mix of buildings including a splendid Victorian black-painted timber dwelling with ornate ironwork called Ivy Castle, a small shanty-style cottage, and the brick and glass houses of the Aquarius development. Unlike many of the inhabited islands further upstream where the houses are often built cheek by jowl, most of Eel Pie's homes have decent garden areas with abundant foliage

Passport to Eelpiland.

separating each dwelling. The main path eventually leads to the island's 'industrial hub': the boatyard and a little alleyway lined with colourful artists' studios that have re-emerged since the fire. Beyond this is the larger nature reserve that occupies almost a quarter of the island at its downstream end. A narrow muddy trail through a dense thicket of very mature trees leads to the tip of the island giving a wonderful view of Ham meadows, and in the far distance the grand Star and Garter Hotel on Richmond Hill. The smaller nature reserve at the upstream end is known as 'the Wilderness', and is home to a colony of sand martins.

On the island's north side is the pleasant blue and white timber building of the Twickenham Rowing Club, one of the oldest clubs on the Thames, with its grand, stepped slipway. Founded in 1860, the club built its headquarters on the island in 1880. Eel Pie is also home to the Richmond Yacht Club. The Thames in London has hardly any working riverfront left, but, much against the odds, the tradition survives here, where the island's last working boatyard, Eel Pie Island Slipways Ltd, is still busy, with all manner of craft awaiting repair.[7] In a classic display of island ingenuity, the boatyard set up a special boat service for local Hindus and Sikhs, enabling them to scatter the ashes of their relatives in the Thames, which remarkably has been declared a tributary of the Ganges for the purpose![8] This service has proved so popular with the large Asian population from neighbouring boroughs, that there is a 'Ganges' funeral at least once a week. Despite its relative normality compared to the heady days of the 1950s and '60s, the island has managed to retain its

Trevor Baylis on Eel Pie Island, 2009.

reputation as a place of refuge for the quirky and unconventional. One Eel Pie family moved from No.14 to No.13 and then to No.10, apparently because they wanted to move nearer to London! In 2005, the island was briefly invaded by writer and presenter Danny Wallace, who intended to claim the territory as his own and form a new country, but order was swiftly restored when his two-man invasion force was routed by local authorities.

The island has had a smattering of famous residents including the first actor to play Dr Who, William Hartnell, and the *Young Ones* actor Nigel Planer. Another is seventy-one-year-old Trevor Baylis OBE, a long-standing resident who invented the clockwork radio on Eel Pie in the 1980s. One of the world's most prolific inventors, Baylis has lived on the island for forty years, where as well as continuing to invent, he works to promote the Trevor Baylis Foundation to encourage and support new inventors.[9] His 1989 prototype clockwork radio was inspired by the needs of the poor in Africa, who, unable to afford batteries, were missing urgent government warnings about the spread of HIV and Aids. Nelson Mandela praised Baylis on behalf of the people of South Africa, so many of whom lived in remote villages but could now get sound without electricity. The same of course applies to the rest of Africa. In an interview in August 2009, Baylis describes how he came to live on Eel Pie:

I had a passion as a young man for jazz and the best club in West London was the Eel Pie Jazz Club on Eel Pie Island. I used to cycle over as a lad and got to see everyone from George Melly to Acker Bilk. I vowed to live at this idyllic spot, as soon as I could afford to make the move. By 1970 I had the money and bought a plot of land. I built a one-bedroom, two-storey house by myself. I've been here ever since and still have to pinch myself to believe I've got a house right on the Thames with my own mooring.[10]

Today this willow-shrouded sanctuary is home to a wide social spectrum of people, who nonetheless form a tight-knit and sociable community. They are immensely proud of their island home and its unique history and are famed for their great island parties which serve as powerful bonding events. Although its glory days are long past, Eel Pie's contribution to the development of popular music and its reputation as the spawning ground of many of the world's most influential recording artists remains legendary. In April 2009, dignitaries and townsfolk from Twickenham and nearby boroughs gathered to watch the unveiling of a plaque on the riverbank to commemorate the historic evolution of rock and roll that began on Eel Pie, and as a tribute to the music heroes who graced this fascinating island in the 1950s, '60s and early '70s.

NOTES

1   *Richmond and Twickenham Times*, 14 January 1899

2   Van Der Vat, D., and Michele Whitby, *Eel Pie Island* (Frances Lincoln Ltd: 2009) p.37

3   Interview with George Melly in *Time Out London*, 2006, p.14

4   Van Der Vat, D., and Michele Whitby, *op. cit.*, p74

5   *Uncut*, January 2011, p.65

6   Van Der Vat, D., and Michele Whitby, *op. cit.*, p.83

7   *Ibid.*, p.94

8   *Ibid.*, p.99

9   For information on the foundation see: www.trevorbaylisbrands.com

10 Interview with Trevor Baylis in the *Financial Times*, 15 August 2009

6

TWICKENHAM TO KINGSTON

T HIS GROUP OF islands is not situated on one of the most beautiful stretches of the Thames but nevertheless its five islands – three of them inhabited – are unique and interesting. Just before the first island is a recreation ground that was once an island at the foot of Waldegrave Road and Cross Deep. Until 1965 the ground was divided by a parallel channel of the river spanned by a bridge leading onto an island, but as the creek had become silted up, it was filled so as to unify the whole space. The bridge though was left in place and the top of its structure can still be seen marking the edge of the footpath leading down from the entrance to the gardens. The island is now called Radnor Gardens.

At the very tail end of Radnor Gardens is **Swan Island**. This small residential island hugs the Middlesex bank to which it is connected by a small road bridge. The island's residents live in a well-established houseboat community that surrounds the island two to three boats deep. There are sixty houseboats in all. The island itself is almost entirely occupied by the large Newman's Boatyard with its giant covered slipway resembling a huge dark 'mouth'. Originally Swan Island was little more than a mudflat known as Milham's Ait after its owner, a local builder, Harry Milham, who built the island entirely out of clay excavated during the construction of the London Underground's Central Line in the late 1890s. Although these days it is a busy industrial space devoid of any greenery, it is very near to the fashionable and bustling town of Twickenham. Thus, due to its location, Swan Island is a popular and desirable place to live and the houseboats command a relatively high price.

There used to be a small eyot just above Swan Island called Rat Ait that was dredged away in the 1890s. Sixty-eight miles from the sea is Teddington Lock, the biggest lock system on the river, which forms the boundary between the tidal and non-tidal Thames. It is here that fresh water from the west meets the salt water from the east and the Environment Agency takes over control of the Thames from the Port of London Authority. **Teddington Lock Ait** is long and narrow and used to be called Crow Ait until it was incorporated into Teddington Lock. The small skiff lock is on a tree-covered islet called **Angler's Ait**, named after the nearby Angler's Tavern, which dates back to 1795. This island has a beautiful little shingle beach near the huge tumbling bay of the weir. Straddling the next bend in the river is the immensely popular **Trowlock Island**.

This attractive, traffic-free inhabited island, a third of a mile in length, is separated from the Teddington bank by a narrow channel. It is approached off the Kingston Road through a recreation ground, which is a distinctly unprepossessing gateway to such a charming island. The island is accessed over a backwater by a quaint hand-wound wooden chain ferry. Rocque's map of 1748 shows Trowlock Island as a chain of three islands – a larger one known as Swans Nest Ayte, flanked by two smaller ones at each end. A later map shows the upstream islet has disappeared, while the other two have merged into the island we see today. Around the middle of the nineteenth century, the island acquired its present name of Trowlock, after a 'trow': a size of barge averaging between 50–60 tons.

Almost half of the downstream end of the island is given over to a semi-wild garden, with around sixty houseboats moored on both the main river and backwater. The rest of the island is quite densely built up with twenty-nine houses and around fifty residents. The undeveloped part of the island is a delightful balance between cultivated and wild. A path meanders through patches of tall

Swan Island, Twickenham.

grasses and flowers, with small ornamental trees dotted about. It then opens out onto a wide lawned area with a sunken concrete pit for communal bonfires. A little wooded enclave contains a large barbeque and chairs where islanders gather for social events. The developed part of the island is also very pleasant. The grassy path gives way to a narrow tarmac lane flanked on both sides by brightly painted, single-storey, predominantly timber-framed homes, many built in the first decades of the last century.

Given that the island occasionally floods, all the houses are built on brick stilts. During the late nineteenth century and the Edwardian era, the river became a destination for crowds of Londoners who craved a respite from the dust and grime

of the city, and wanted to enjoy the cleanliness and tranquillity of Thames-side islands and meadows. The era of the riverside weekend bungalow had begun, and Trowlock, as one of the islands closest to London, was one of the first to be discovered as a holiday retreat. At first, people would camp, but eventually they acquired small plots on which they built wooden huts that were later rebuilt or extended as chalets and bungalows. It wasn't until the mid-1940s, however, that the island was occupied all year round. Today, Trowlock Island has one of the very last original wooden weekend huts to be seen on the Thames.

At the upstream end of the island are beautifully tended communal gardens, resplendent with roses and flowering shrubs, which lead to the chain ferry.

Alongside the gardens there is a newly renovated building that hosts the Royal Canoe Club, formed in July 1866; it was the first such club in the world. In 1867, Edward, Prince of Wales (later King Edward VII) became commodore of the club, and in 1873, by command of Queen Victoria, the club became the Royal Canoe Club. In 1897, the Club leased some land on Trowlock Island, which it later purchased. The chalet-style timber clubhouse, dated 1866, is still the main base for canoeing on the Thames.

The island is run by volunteers, who, through a company called Trowlock Island Ltd, manage the shared infrastructure of the island, and earn an income from mooring charges. The company's board of directors is elected by the shareholders: each bungalow or plot of land carries with it a number of shares so that all house owners, including the Royal Canoe Club, collectively own the company. By the late 1940s enough people lived on the island year round to install a permanent raft as a ferry, and in 1948 a license fee for the ferry was agreed with the Thames Conservancy. The original fee to passengers riding back and forth across the tiny width of the Thames to the island was tuppence. This went up over the years to reach £3.77 in the early 1970s, where it settled for decades. Then in 2001 the Environment Agency (EA) carried out assessments and came up with a new license fee of £5,000 per year, based on precedents set downstream from Teddington Lock, even though Trowlock Island is situated upstream from the lock.

The islanders were understandably shocked by this 'extortionate' fee slammed on their charming little ferry, labelling it 'the most expensive ferry in Europe', if judged by usage and distance. Recognising that £3.77 was ridiculously low, Trowlock Island Ltd offered to settle at £1,000, but the agency refused the offer. In January 2005 the islanders mounted a legal challenge against the fee, to which the EA responded by taking the issue to the High Court, even though the islanders, with their meagre funds, felt the matter could have been settled in the small claims court. 'This is a little organisation fighting a massive monster' John Bazalgette, who has lived on the island since 1969 and is a descendant of the creator of the London sewer system, told the *Richmond and Twickenham Times*. Meanwhile, the EA argued that: 'The cost of maintaining the River Thames as a public waterway far exceeds the income received from river users. This is part of a river-wide review to get the balance right between those who use the river and the community who have to subsidise it through their taxes.'[1] The matter was eventually settled at £100 per household, i.e. £2,900 altogether.

Aside from issues with the EA, life on Trowlock is very quiet and peaceful. In summer a barbecue is held in the island's garden, sometimes with a band playing (Ronnie Wood from The Rolling Stones and Status Quo's Rick Parfitt have come along and strummed a guitar in the past). Usually, however, this end of the island remains utterly peaceful and provides a roaming ground for Trowlock's large population of cats and dogs.[2] The island as a whole has a wonderful community spirit and is obviously a place that people cherish and care for. As one resident explained, despite the risk of floods, 'we put up with it because it's a very mellow existence and the island is so idyllic in summer.'

Shortly after leaving Trowlock, directly opposite Canbury Gardens Park lies **Steven's Eyot** and accompanying islet.

This eyot is in fact two islands, the first being a tiny, almost circular, unnamed islet that is home to a colony of ducks and several splendid trees. Immediately after this comes the main Steven's Eyot. A small, thin, uninhabited island, flat as a sheet of paper, it is a favourite of boating crowds because it is leased from the EA by the Small Boat Club (SBC). From April until October the island is a hive of activity with the coming and going of all manner of small craft. Since 1984 the SBC has had a jetty on the Surrey bank from which a ferry service operates at weekends for members to reach the island; on weekdays they have to row themselves across.

Trowlock Island chain ferry, Teddington.

An old pioneer chalet on Trowlock Island, Teddington.

The island appears to have changed its shape quite dramatically over the years. In Rocque's 1745 map of the Thames, Steven's Eyot is shown as three nameless islands: one relatively large and two slightly smaller. In 1840 the islands were owned by George Burchett, who leased them to William Parkhurst, a basket maker who grew osiers there. By 1865, however, maps show a group of four islands of varying sizes, mostly marshy with a few trees, but again with no name. The aits were much larger during this period than they are now. They have always suffered from flooding, which may account for their diminished size today.

In 1872 the islands became the site of Kingston's first public swimming area when, following complaints about nude bathing in the river, a canvas screen was erected around part of the islands 'for public bathing'. The 'public', however, didn't include women and children, who were forbidden to make use of it. By 1895 just two islands remained: the larger one was now called Tathim's Island and was the shape of a boomerang, and the small islet at the downstream end was called Tea Island. By 1912 the islands had become known as Steven's Eyots, after a local boatman who built a boathouse on the larger island.

Up until the First World War, both islands were very popular with weekend rowers having picnic parties. By some accounts these seem to have been quite lively affairs. In 1917 Thacker noticed to his relief 'that the plague of gramophones on the islands on Sundays had been silenced by Kingston Corporation.' By the 1960s the islands had changed shape yet again, with the little Tea Island having now disappeared into the river, and the larger island having broken into two, leaving the tiny islet to the downstream end. This is pretty much how we find Steven's Eyot today, with the main island ringed with willow trees that have been neatly clipped at the bottom to allow boating activity beneath.

The Small Boat Club was formed in 1953 by the splendidly named Arthur Rowbottom and Jacko Jackson. In 1960 the eyot was leased from the Thames Conservancy (now the Environment Agency). While sailing boats and their owners were initially part of the club, the SBC, with its attractive clubhouse, is now mainly orientated around powered craft, although some members still keep skiffs and kayaks. The club organises a number of boating and river-related events from their island base, which is complete with an inviting picnic and barbeque area. Membership is open to those with or without boats, but for many, just having use of the island as their 'secret garden', is reason enough to belong.[3] In all, Steven's Eyot, together with its little islet, is a real feature in this otherwise fairly nondescript section of the Thames.

Passing under Kingston Bridge and up to Hart's Boatyard in Surbiton, we reach a fair-sized island called **Raven's Ait**.

Kingston Boat Club on Raven's Ait, 1896.

This imposing and somewhat intimidating island of around an acre in size, lies almost in the centre of the river. It is shaped like a small ship, and is accessed by a private ferry. The northern half of the island is developed with various sized timber-clad buildings, while the southern part is mainly tree-covered with a small garden. What makes it rather menacing is its fortress-like appearance. In the late nineteenth century the island had been raised considerably by the dumping of waste soil, and has since been well protected by high, reinforced camp-shedding, on top of which is some serious metal fencing that surrounds the whole island. The reason for all of this is not at all apparent.

The island has a long recorded history. Thames picks, used for felling trees in the Middle Stone Age, have been discovered on submerged land on Raven's Ait. According to local historian June Sampson, the island is thought to be the setting for the creation of the Treaty of Kingston, which saved England from the prospect of submitting to total French control in the thirteenth century. She explains that the policies of King John were so unpopular that in 1216 the English barons offered the crown to Louis, eldest son of the King of France, who accepted and soon controlled half the shires in the country, and might have taken them all had John not died suddenly. With John safely gone, the nobles now wanted only to rally around his nine-year-old son and see him crowned Henry III. But how to get rid of the foreign prince they had invited to become king? The problem was finally solved in 1217, when Louis and the barons rowed to an island in the Thames, almost certainly Raven's Ait, where they thrashed out the Treaty of Kingston.[4]

From 1603–17 the island was known as Moorehill, and was opposite a meadow on the bank with the unfortunate name of Raven's Arse. Both island and meadow were then owned by the Bailiffs and Freemen of Kingston, who planted osiers and other reeds for commercial use.

In 1640 the island was owned by a William Moorcock of Laleham and was known as Moorcock's Ayte. By 1649 it was recorded as one acre of meadowland known as Raven's Arse, and in 1745 Rocque's map also calls the island Raven's Arse. The island was used as meadowland and osier beds right up until the middle of the nineteenth century. In 1840 it was owned by Alexander Raphael, an MP and leading Roman Catholic who was responsible for building St Raphael's church.

In 1858 Kingston Rowing Club leased the island, where it held colourful amateur regattas. By this time the island had a boathouse and had been renamed Raven's Ait due to its increasing popularity as a rowing venue, and to dispense with its previously embarrassing name. An 1865 map shows the island with another small islet at its upstream end which has long since disappeared. In 1909 the island was sold to Hart's Boat Builder's for £4,000. Over the next eighty years, it was leased to various institutions, including the Navy League, a charity responsible for the Sea Cadet Corps and the Girl's Nautical Training Corps, until 1989 when the island was bought by Kingston Borough for £1.4 million, after local residents feared that the late Robert Maxwell was going to buy the island and build a huge house and helipad on it.

For the next twenty years the island was run as a recreation centre, and in 1995 it was leased by Raven's Ait Ltd, who turned it into a hospitality and conference centre. In 2008 disagreement arose over whether the island was private or common land. Kingston Council argued that it was private, in the sense that it belonged to the borough, which then leased it to private companies or individuals. Many of the inhabitants of Kingston, however, insisted that the island was common land belonging to all the people of Kingston, and therefore should not be privatised. Things came to a head in December, 2008 when Raven's Ait Ltd went into liquidation.

In the meantime, the island had become neglected and was in a sorry state when, in March 2009, a dozen eco-protestors arrived by barge and promptly took over the ait in support of the assertion that it was 'common land'. Within days they had tidied up the conference buildings, restored the gardens and invited locals to come and picnic in the island's garden. They won the support of many Kingstonians by declaring their aim of turning the island into an eco-conference centre. This was all too much for Kingston Council, which on March 23 obtained a court order to evict the squatters. Meanwhile, the island's new inhabitants had set up a cinema, started music workshops for children and put on dance, music, and theatre performances.[5]

Thus, for the first time, local people were able to enjoy one of Kingston's greatest river assets, but it was a short-lived experience as the eco-warriors were eventually evicted on 1 May 2009. Although some older, more conservative local people had initially been alarmed by the unorthodox approach and appearance of the squatters, even they had to acknowledge that something positive for the local community had been created on Raven's Ait. After much consultation, the island was eventually awarded to Osie Stewart, the Olympic sailing medallist. At the time of writing, the island's future will be that of a community-based water centre, offering facilities and training for rowing, canoeing, sailing and other river-based activities.

Carrying on upstream, just past Thames Ditton Marina, lie a small group of islands, one of which has an intruiguing history.

NOTES

1   *Richmond and Twickenham Times*, 14 October 2005

2   *The Times*, 20 August 2004

3   For more information about the Small Boat Club see: www.smallboatclub.co.uk

4   Sampson, June, *Surrey Comet*, 31 December 2008

5   'Squatters on Thames Island', *Time Out London*, 14 April 2009

7

THE THAMES DITTON ISLANDS

THERE IS ONLY one island and two little islets in this group; the first of which is **Boyle Farm Island.**

This tiny wooded islet is the second largest of the three Ditton islands. It is named after an historic mansion situated almost directly opposite it on the Surrey bank. There is only one building on the island, a black and white timbered house called Grebe Cottage, which is surrounded by a secluded garden with an attractive boathouse fronting a tiny slipway. The house is barely visible above the trees and with its little front garden, picket fence and delapidated rustic bench facing the water, it is as near to perfection as any island dwelling can be.

Sandwiched between Boyle Farm Island and the next island is **Swan Island**. This even more diminutive, almost circular ait, the smallest of the three islands, resembles a swan's nest, particularly in winter when the leafless trees expose the island's rim of woven roots. It is so small that its only building, the old ferryman's hut, seems like a giant cukoo in the nest. The hut, which has recently been restored, sits squarely in the centre of the little ait and is almost completely hidden when the trees are in leaf.

Swan Island virtually touches the largest island in this group, which is also one of the most popular residential islands on the entire river: **Thames Ditton Island**.

This banana-shaped island is situated directly opposite the 600-year-old Olde Swan pub, and is one of the most densely populated on the Thames. Its popularity is due mainly to its location: close to both Kingston town centre and to Thames Ditton with its mainline station and links to Waterloo. The most striking thing about the island is the very attractive ornate suspension footbridge that connects it to the Surrey bank. It was the building of this bridge in 1939 that really opened up the island as a place for permanent occupation. As well as providing passage on foot, it also carries water, electricity and gas onto the island, and takes the sewage away to the town drains.[1] The bridge has a toll gate to which the inhabitants have a key.

The island is 350 yards long, with forty-seven houses, almost all built on stilts, and a population of around 100. The mainstream side of the island has stunning views looking across to the grounds of Hampton Court Park. Approaching the island from downstream, it resembles the prow of a ship with a sturdy brick wall above the camp-shedding surrounding its pointed tip. Before the arrival of Hampton Court Palace this part of Surrey was largely uninhabited marshy wetlands, but over time people working at the palace began to settle and live in Thames Ditton and use the island as a crossing point over to the palace.

According to local resident Michael Russell, as late as 1895 the island was then not much more than an overgrown, muddy, tree-clad hump, but the skiffs of the day trippers from Kingston moored there to enjoy a riverside picnic. In the early part of the twentieth century a number of holiday chalets were built on the island. Gradually the attractions of the waterside location drew more and more people, so that by 1930 the whole of the island's perimeter was covered in wooden bungalows. Originally leased from the island's owner, the publican at the Olde Swan, all of the houses had passed into freehold ownership by 1963.[2]

One of the more outrageous characters to be associated with any Thames island is the notorious swindler Maundy Gregory, an extraordinary conman and purveyor

Swan Island and Boyle Farm Island, Thames Ditton.

Ariel photo of Thames Ditton Island, c.1934.

chalet called Vanity Fair on Thames Ditton Island. He and his friends Mr and Mrs Rosse enjoyed entertaining their London friends on the island and generally relaxing on the river. Mrs Rosse eventually separated from her husband and despite Gregory being homosexual, he and Mrs Rosse set up home together in a mansion flat opposite London's Hyde Park. Mrs Rosse had received a handsome financial settlement from her husband and to protect some of his own assets, Gregory transferred some into Edith's name, including the title of his chalet on Thames Ditton Island. As a consequence he took a keen interest in helping Mrs Rosse with her financial affairs, but it seems to the neglect of his own financial situation, which by 1932 was looking bleak as his debts increased and his scheming began to catch up with him.

In the late summer of 1932, Mrs Rosse began to suffer from strange bouts of sickness. On 19 August she feared she was dying and summoned Gregory, to whom she then dictated her will, which was witnessed by her housekeeper and her doctor. She left her entire estate to Maundy Gregory. The next few weeks saw Mrs Rosse deteriorate until she eventually died on 14 September. Her death certificate cited 'Cerebral haemorrhage and chronic Bright's Disease' as the cause of death. According to Cullen, however, a year beforehand Maundy had confided to a friend

of honours and influence. During the Edwardian era Gregory set himself up as an honours broker and was on intimate terms with people at the very pinnacle of the establishment: from cabinet ministers, generals and admirals to senior clergy and civil servants. As his biographer Tom Cullen notes: 'Gregory managed to build a magic aura around himself as one who also enjoyed royal favour. Yet in time he came to be feared by the very men who had befriended him as The Man Who Knew Too Many Secrets.'[3]

Gregory was not the first, but he was by some distance the most successful and infamous honours broker of his time. By the early 1930s, when his notoriety had made him a liability to those in power, Gregory had resorted to outright fraud, selling 'non-existent' honours. For the purposes of this book, however, it is not Gregory's shady honours dealings that are of interest, but rather the fact that he was suspected of murder following the sudden death of his friend, a middle-aged actress named Edith Marion Rosse, in September 1932.

In the summer of 1910 Gregory's profile on the London scene was rising, and in order to escape the city at weekends, he took a ninety-year lease on a little wooden

Maundy Gregory's chalet, Vanity Fair, on Thames Ditton Island.

Edith Rosse and Maundy Gregory at Thames Ditton Island.

that he knew how to commit the perfect murder. He had apparently obtained some South American curare, a poison which relaxed the abdominal muscles to the point where breathing stopped. If the body was then immersed in water all trace of the poison would disappear as curare was soluble.[4]

Although the subsequent autopsy found no trace of poison in Mrs Rosse's body, and the inquest into her death recorded an open verdict, doubts began to emerge. Gregory's dire financial situation provided a strong motive for murder, and also of concern were the details of her bizarre funeral arrangements. Apparently, she had told Gregory that she had always wanted to be buried near her beloved Thames. Why then did Gregory not have her buried in the parish church of St Nicholas at Thames Ditton where she had spent so many happy times, and indeed where she was entitled to be buried as she and her husband had once owned a house in Thames Ditton? Instead, Gregory searched the Thames Valley high and low until he found a graveyard over 30 miles upriver at Bisham, literally within inches of the river and known to flood in winter. If that wasn't odd enough, he then insisted that the coffin be lead-lined and that the grave be as shallow as possible. His most peculiar request, however, was that the coffin be left unsealed; when asked about sealing it, Maundy had replied: 'Oh no, that would seem too final.'[5]

Having spent every summer for the past twenty-two years on Thames Ditton Island, Gregory was very familiar with floods. On occasions the river has completely covered the island in several feet of water. Notably, this flooding occurred in 1928 and again in 1930. Mrs Rosse was finally buried a few feet from the banks of the Thames in Bisham churchyard where the water seeps through the gravel bank, and rises and falls with the tides by capillary action, resulting in a continuous flushing action.[6] The following year, in 1933, justice finally caught up with Gregory and he stood trial at Bow Street Magistrates' Court where, on 21 February he was sentenced to imprisonment in Wormwood Scrubs prison for peddling honours. On his release he settled in France, where he died in September 1941. There was certainly enough circumstantial evidence surrounding the suspicious death of his 'dearest friend' Mrs Edith Rosse to lead many to believe that Gregory should have been tried for murder. Today, Mrs Rosse's watery grave can still be seen perched on the river bank by beautiful Bisham church.

Vanity Fair today is an attractive timber-clad house but it may never have quite shaken off the shadows of Maundy Gregory and Edith Rosse. Island resident Sarah Blackburn, keeping an eye on the bungalow while the owner was abroad, always hated going in at night. Shortly before moving out, the owner reported catching a glimpse of an apparition – a woman in the garden. 'She wore a long old-fashioned dress,' Mrs Blackburn recalled, 'and one instinctively thinks of poor Edith.'[7]

Despite its shady past, 'the island', as it is known by its inhabitants, is a pleasant, colourful place albeit perhaps a little crowded, as the homes with their small

Maundy Gregory.

Bisham church with Mrs Edith Rosse's grave at the water's edge.

gardens jostle cheek by jowl facing either the mainstream river or the Surrey bank over the narrow backwater. Having crossed the bridge, a small park-like garden leads to a lane running the length of the island between the mostly timber-framed houses. In the 1960s, the islanders formed a limited company, whose directors are elected by the shareholders of the island, in order to maintain the bridge, the little public garden and other island services. Flooding is still the most feared issue for islanders. In recent years the island has been seriously flooded three times, in October 1999, January 2000 and again in January 2003, when the highest flood levels of modern times were recorded and in order to walk along the island's path you needed chest waders. Despite this very real and dangerous threat, the resilient residents remain wedded to their island home.

NOTES

1   Russell, M., 'A Resident's View', www.thamesditton.com, 2000

2   *Ibid.*

3   Cullen, T., *Maundy Gregory: Purveyor of Honours* (London: The Bodley Head, 1974) p.9

4   *Ibid.*, p.175

5   Cook, A., *Cash for Honours: The Story of Maundy Gregory* (Stroud: The History Press, 2008) p.235

6   Cullen, T., *op. cit.,* p.214

7   Wilkes, R., *The Telegraph*, 10 February 2001

Mrs Rosse's grave, Bisham churchyard.

THE HAMPTON COURT ISLANDS

MEANWHILE, THE RIVER trundles on until it passes a point where the River Ember enters the Thames opposite Hampton Court. The little park that juts out into the Thames at this point was known as **Cigarette Island**.

This is another non-island that warrants a brief mention because Hampton Court Station stands upon what was, before 1930, a bona fide island called Cigarette Island. Local historian Rowland Baker explains that at that time, the River Mole entered the Thames approximately where the present bridge now stands. In the early 1930s, when Hampton Court Way was constructed to form an approach to the new bridge, the Mole was diverted into the River Ember above East Molesey Mill, and this part of the Mole was filled in. In 1843 it was called 'Davis Ait' after the family who at one time kept the Castle Inn. The present name derives from a houseboat called *Cigarette* that used to be moored here in the 1920s, along with many others.[1] In 1935 Cigarette Island was cleared of its houseboat community and was opened to the public as a municipal park. Today, it is a popular and attractive spot with a great view of Hampton Court.

Passing under Hampton Court Bridge on the right bank, there was once a tiny two tree covered islet called Wren's Ait, after the famous architect, Sir Christopher Wren, who lived in a house with a garden that backed onto it. The islet was dredged away in 1931. Almost opposite the site of this lost little ait is Molesey Lock, opened in 1815, from where you can walk across the long weir footbridge onto **Ash Island**. It is pure coincidence that Ash should follow Cigarette Island.

This large, inhabited pear-shaped island lies in the centre of the river. It is approximately 4 acres in size and was once part of a group of five islands of which only three remain. There are two weirs at either end of Ash Island, and these give it a very dramatic aspect. Consequently, there is a difference of several feet in the water level on each side, and an amazing sound of thundering water from all corners of the island. As late as the middle of the nineteenth century, the channel between Ash Island and neighbouring Tagg's Island was so narrow that it was possible to jump across it, but later when the main weir of Molesey Lock was constructed, the backwash caused erosion, and much of the south-east tip was washed away and the present 'Hog Hole' formed between the two islands. Around seventy people live on Ash Island in two houses, one boathouse and around thirty houseboats. At the southern corner of the island is a busy boatyard. Most of the ait is densely covered in a mixed array of trees, many of them ash, hence the island's present name.

In the past it has been known as Mr Clay's Ait, Angler's Ait, Harvey's Ait, Ashen Ait and Robinson Crusoe Island. The latter name could still apply today with the island's thickly wooded interior quickly enveloping the visitor and shutting off the outside world. In the late 1840s, an island tenant, Mr Clay, built a wooden beer house to provide refreshment for the increasing numbers of fishermen and boaters who were discovering this stretch of the Thames. A few years later, another tenant, Mr Joseph Harvey, extended the beer house with tea rooms and a skittle alley, calling it the 'Angler's Retreat'. Due to persistent flooding, however, he moved his business from Ash Island onto the larger, neighbouring Tagg's Island. In 1866 Molesey Boat Club was established on the island before it too moved to larger mainland premises in 1899.

At one time the island was much lower than it is today and was often overrun by floods. In 1844 it was almost washed away. The island's present height is due

Ash Island in around 1950.

Ash Island, Hampton Court.

The original Molesey Boat Club building of 1866 on Ash Island.

THAMES VALLEY *from the Air.*
MOLESEY LOCK, TAGGS ISLAND AND KARSINO.

Ariel view of densely wooded Ash and Tagg's islands in the late 1920s. Note the tiny islet to the right of Tagg's Island that was dredged away to make room for a bridge over to the island in 1941.

to two factors: firstly, between 1854 and 1856 the water works and filter beds at Hampton were constructed, and the excavated superfluous earth was deposited on various nearby aits, including Ash Island, raising its height to a level which reduced the threat of flooding. Also, the weir at Molesey Lock was rebuilt in 1882 after it was damaged in the Great Flood of 1877. At this time two large portions of Ash Island were purchased and dredged away, the spoil being spread over the rest of the island to further raise its level. The tail of the island was also cut away to enable the weir to be lengthened.[2]

At the beginning of the twentieth century, swimming in the Thames became increasingly popular. It was, however, exclusively a male pastime and women walking along the towpaths became, understandably, highly agitated by the sight of nude men and boys cavorting around in the water. Therefore, the local councils established bathing stations in some secluded areas of the river, and in 1901 one was opened on Ash Island. In 1947 a local insurance broker, George Henry Booker, bought Ash Island and then sold off various portions. George was president of Molesey Boat Club and once or twice a year he road his horse Tony across the river to the island. Apparently, he did this as a publicity stunt for the boat club, as he gave prior notification of the event to the local press. Today, the shed next to the Long Boathouse is still referred to as 'Tony's Shed', as that is where the horse was stabled when he stayed on the island.[3] George died in 1966.

Today, the thick tree cover and natural vegetation in the undisturbed interior of this beautiful secluded island provides a refuge for nesting water fowl and other smaller creatures such as rare stag beetles and hedgehogs. It is therefore an important ecology site as well as providing a striking central feature in the river.

Directly above Ash Island lies the fascinating **Tagg's Island**. After Eel Pie, Tagg's Island is probably the most famous and certainly one of the most interesting islands on the Thames. It lies opposite the old Hurst Park Racecourse and Molesey Cricket Ground on the Surrey bank, and Bushy Park on the Middlesex bank. This large inhabited island covers 5 acres, and is a quarter of a mile in length. It is a highly sought-after place to live with a thriving houseboat community and a magical lagoon at its centre. The sixty or so dwellings are mostly double-decked houseboats moored around the perimeter of the island; some are quite grandiose, others more modest, with another twenty smaller, single-decked homes moored in the lagoon, all attached to piles driven into the riverbed. Although they are called boats, it is unlikely that any are actually capable of independent steerage. As all the dwellings are on water, the island itself has been given over to decent-sized gardens and a communal park with a small woodland area, which is used for the islanders' many

Tagg's Island, c.1998.

social events. Part of Tagg's popularity is due to the fact that this is one of the few Thames islands where you can actually drive straight up to your house over a solid road bridge connected to the Middlesex bank.

Tagg's Island has a long recorded history, which has for the most part been tainted with frustration and despair. Until as late as the 1980s this was an island of dashed hopes and lost fortunes, as every entrepreneur who set up a business on the island went bankrupt within a few years. Local legend says that this is the result of an old gypsy curse. In Rocque's map of 1745, Tagg's Island is shown without a name, but by the early 1800s it was called Garrick's Lower Eyot, so it was most probably owned, or at least rented, by the celebrated actor David Garrick (1717–79), who owned a villa on the nearby Middlesex bank and an island a little way upstream that was then called Garrick's Upper Eyot. By the 1830s, however, it was known as Walnut Tree Island, and was a wilderness and haunt of wildlife, including otters.

The development of the island did not begin until 1850 when it was bought by a local property developer, Francis Kent, and was subsequently called Kent's Ait. When Kent purchased the island it was populated by a number of squatter families who made a precarious living by cutting osiers that they then peeled, bleached in the sun and made into baskets. After Kent had them evicted, legend has it that some were gypsies who cursed him, saying that nobody connected with the island would ever prosper.[4] In time this was to prove extremely prophetic. By the 1850s the growth in popularity of angling brought picnic parties and fishermen to the island. To capitalise on this, in 1852 local businessman Joseph Harvey, who ran the Angler's Retreat on Ash Island, rented a part of Tagg's island from Kent, where he built a new beer house and skittle alley called the Island Hotel. He couldn't make it prosper, however, and left the island in 1862.

In 1868 Kent leased another part of the island to a boat builder called Thomas George Tagg, who eventually leased the whole island, and in September 1872 he rebuilt the Island Hotel as the Thames Hotel. In excavating the foundations of the hotel, workmen came across the skull of an extinct species of goat and the jawbone of a large boar's head. Before long, Tagg had transformed the island into a popular pleasure resort that attracted wealthy patrons not only to the island but also to the surrounding area. In 1882 a wealthy local landowner erected the famous Swiss Chalet opposite Tagg's Island, which still stands on the Middlesex bank. This exotic structure was dismantled and brought from Switzerland and then up the Thames in three barges and was then reassembled in the gardens of a house called Riverholme, which no longer exists, to house and entertain guests.

Tagg's Island became a Mecca for practically everyone in high society, including royalty, actors, literary folk, artists and musicians. During the season the houseboats were covered with flowers, and in the evening their beauty was enhanced by thousands of lanterns and fairy lamps. To gaze on this wonderful sight, then unequalled anywhere else, crowds thronged the towpath. But Tagg's pride in his island was short lived, for in June 1897, then aged fifty-seven, Tom Tagg caught a cold and died within three days. His son George was left to carry on.[5] For a year or two all went well, but following the worst flood in Hampton's history, followed by the Boer War and the death of Queen Victoria, people's spirits were dampened and trade began to fall away. In 1903 the hotel was put into the hands of a receiver and continued to be run by the creditors as Tagg's Island Hotel Ltd, but with little success.

When Tagg's original lease expired in 1911, George Tagg sold the hotel to Mr Fred Karno. This was the stage name of Frederick Westcott, a theatrical producer born in Exeter in 1866, who made his name by staging a series of spectacular and original comic shows. Having trained as a gymnast, appearing at fairgrounds and travelling circuses, Karno was eventually called to stand in for the slapstick act The Three Karnos at the Metropolitan theatre in the Edgware Road. Thus, The Three Karnos were born. Soon Karno gave up appearing to concentrate on organising a string of touring companies that included acts by Charlie Chaplin, Stan Laurel, Will Hay and Flanagan and Allen.[6] With the increase in the popularity of the cinema, however, Karno's style of music hall entertainment had waned. He hoped the Tagg's Island venture would revive his flagging fortunes.

In June 1913 he opened the Karsino Hotel. Historian Roland Baker describes how everything imaginable was done to tempt wealthy patrons to the island. In a bid to bring 'the Continental atmosphere upriver' there was a Dutch garden and a German beer garden. There were tennis, croquet, bowls and badminton

The Casino Hotel, Tagg's Island, 1927.

Fred Karno's magnificent houseboat the Astoria *now moored at Hampton.*

Houseboats on Tagg's Island, 2011.

Houseboats on the lagoon, Tagg's Island.

courts and it had a ballroom that could fit 350 people. The Karno publicity machine went to work plastering the whole metropolis with posters, so that no Londoner was left in any doubt as to what was taking place on 'Tagg's Island in the glorious River Thames'. Revellers flocked there: indeed so many thousands packed onto the island that at one point it was impossible to move, and many thousands more were left to line the banks on either side of the river.[7] Thus, for a time, the Karsino was monumentally successful. Billed as 'the finest and most luxurious River Hotel in Europe', there had never been anything like it before, and for one glorious year the Karsino reached an unprecedented pinnacle of riverside opulence and glamour.

When the money began to flow, Fred bought a houseboat on Tagg's Island. Before long, however, this boat was not deemed grand enough. He had to have something far more magnificent. Thus in 1913, at enormous cost, he had built the biggest and most luxurious houseboat on the river – a veritable floating palace, christened the *Astoria* – all others paled into insignificance beside it.[8] This craft is still afloat, now lying a short distance upriver, and is still remarkable for her rich panelled cabins and marble ballrooms. After Karno's day she became the river home of Vesta Victoria, the music hall star famous for her song 'Daddy Wouldn't Buy me a Bow-Wow'. Local tradition has it that Chaplin had his first audition with Karno, which led to his great stage and film career, aboard this boat.[9] In 1986 the *Astoria* was bought by Dave Gilmore of Pink Floyd, who converted it into a recording studio and in 2005 recorded his album *On an Island* on it.

As long as the unpredictable English weather held up, people flocked to Tagg's Island. But the rain was Karno's biggest enemy. He took out an insurance policy to insure against rain spoiling his events, but the terms were more advantageous to the insurance company, and in the single week when Karno did collect a big sum, one of his employees ran off with the takings.[10] Then, in little more than a year from the opening date, the First World War broke out. Although the Karsino stayed open, it ran at a continued loss. When peace came, few had money to spend on entertainment. Those that did took to the new hobby of motoring rather than rowing and punting. The river had lost its allure in favour of the road, and the effect on the island was inevitable. Yet Fred struggled on, until three summers of bad weather, 1922–5, drove him to bankruptcy.

The image of Fred Karno's army quickly passed into English folklore. Wittingly or otherwise, Karno's name became a synonym for anything alluding to the comic, but with a more pathetic connotation. There was something strangely prophetic in that popular marching song of the First World War: 'We are Fred Karno's Army, as you can plainly see. We cannot shoot, we cannot fight, what bloody use are we?' Fred Karno ended his days as a manager of an off-licence in Dorset. He died on 17 September 1941, aged seventy-five. The immortality Karno so desperately sought was inherited by his most famous protégé, Charlie Chaplin.[11]

In 1926 a new owner, Mr Beaumont Alexander, took over the Karsino Hotel, renaming it the Casino. He planted palm trees and brought in sand to create a beach. A painting of this period called *Tagg's Island* by Sir Alfred Munnings depicts a fashionable picnic on the island. Two years later, however, Mr Alexander had lost all his money, and in June 1928, the fifth man to run a business on Tagg's Island (and the fifth to regret it), Mr Herbert Cyril, took over. His opening night at Tagg's Island outdid even those of his immediate predecessors, but six months later he too was bankrupt. The Gypsy's curse appeared to be working overtime. In May 1930 another London impresario, Mr. A.E. Bundy, took over the island. His vision was to turn the island into a Continental riviera. The Casino was renamed the Thames Riviera and incorporated a covered tennis court and a magnificent skating rink. Like all of its predecessors, Thames Riviera had a grand opening celebration on 22 June 1930 but within six weeks the luckless Mr Bundy was also declared bankrupt.[12] The lease then passed to a firm called Tagg's Island Properties Ltd, who continued to run the hotel until the Second World War. In 1941 AC Cars bought the freehold of the island and after turning the magnificent skating rink and covered tennis courts into a munitions factory, constructed a road bridge connected to the northern bank and built their famous sky-blue three-wheeled invalid cars there for war victims. Sadly, the rest of the island became neglected and overgrown.

Following sixteen years of tranquillity, virtually the only calm period in its history, the island was sold in 1956 to Mr J. Rennie for £75,000. His many schemes for the island, which included skyscraper flats and bowling alleys, were all refused, and so in 1965 he entered into agreement with a Mr Ramsawak Doon Pandit to sell the freehold of the island for £150,000, plus a further £30,000 for the hotel. But within a few weeks the deal fell through due to an anonymous tip-off to Thames River Police that the bridge linking the island to the mainland was unsafe. Mr. Pandit, who had previously joked about his 'voodoo island', claimed he had been misled and refused to pay the outstanding balance from the sale. A complicated legal battle ensued. While this was going on the bridge duly collapsed into the river.[13] Mr Pandit was then sued by his creditors, and the new owner, American entrepreneur Leon Bronesky, put in a planning application to pull down the old hotel and build a new luxurious hotel, five storeys high with swimming pools and a marina plus a new two-lane bridge.

Despite strong opposition from the houseboat dwellers, the plan was approved by Richmond Council in February 1971. On 15 March 1971, the dilapidated old hotel was finally demolished amidst an orgy of nostalgia for the old building, and the remains of the buildings were destroyed by a number of disastrous fires. Just prior to its demolition the old hotel was used as a film location for Stanley Kubrick's film *A Clockwork Orange*, where Alex and his droogs ambush Billy Boy's gang. On demolition day Mr Bronesky invited many stars of British music hall society to a

Duck Eyot off Tagg's Island.

farewell lunch in Karsino's old dancehall. A host of then celebrities attended, including Roy Hudd, Jimmy Jewel, Beryl Reid, Roy Kinnear, Bill Oddie, Tim Brooke-Taylor, Graham Chapman and Eric Idle, an event that was recorded by the BBC. Thus, what *The Times* described as 'one of the strangest buildings in Britain', came tumbling down, and an era of British entertainment history was but a pile of rubble.

For a number of reasons Mr Bronesky's grandiose plans failed to materialise and in 1975 he too was declared bankrupt. The island's new owners, Clarebrooke Holdings, put forward yet more plans for a great number of flats and a restaurant. Yet more planning applications were continually rejected whilst the island became a desolate overgrown wilderness, a sad relic of its former glory, with absolutely nothing to show for the fortunes that had been poured into it. What was really required for this unique Thames island was a quiet, settled and respectable future. The inertia continued until the end of the 1970s by which time much of the centre of the island was a messy clutter of scrubby bushes, patches of concrete, a few rotting sheds and steps which led nowhere. Ironically, the island once again faced the prospect of being occupied by squatters over 120 years after Mr Kent had evicted his. By this time, several families were living on houseboats moored along the island's perimeter.

Gradually the island reverted back to nature, becoming almost impenetrable by the time two of the houseboat residents, Gerry and Gillian Braban, bought the freehold of the island in 1980 from Richmond Council for £158,000 and formed Tagg's Island Limited to rescue the island from dereliction. In a Herculean manner they then set about dramatically revitalising the island by creating a large lagoon in the centre for twenty houseboats, whose mooring fees would fund the construction of a new road bridge. This was a visionary project as tons of soil had to be dug from the middle of the island and heaps of rubbish and debris was also cleared. Mr Braban designed and built a vacuum sewage system, laid new gas and electric mains, new water pipes and an underground TV ariel. He also planted innumerable palm trees and exotic shrubs, which today help give the island its distinctive Continental look. Gerry Braban died in 1993 and a sundial was erected in his honour on the river's north bank.

Since then the island has settled into much deserved tranquillity. On its banks, what were quite basic houseboats until fairly recently have now largely been superseded by opulent, spacious, state-of-the-art floating homes. Although most of the great Victorian and Edwardian boats have disappeared, Tagg's Island remains a beautiful, peaceful place with its enchanting and colourful lagoon, and an open, spacious feel that is lacking on many other inhabited islands. The gypsy's curse finally seems to have been lifted as today's islanders appear relatively contented and secure.

A few feet upstream from Tagg's is a tiny islet called **Duck Eyot**. This little ait was once known as 'Swan's Nest Island'. Old maps show the island as being much larger than it is today. To prevent its erosion, and to keep the channel clear for navigation, the Thames Conservancy protected this islet and the head of Tagg's with a barrier of camp-shedding.14 The islet has just three large weeping willows and is usually full of sleeping ducks until someone moors up alongside to have a picnic.

NOTES

1   Baker, R.G.M., *Thameside Molesey* (Barracuda Books Ltd,1989) p.15

2   Baker, *Ibid.*, p.43

3   Ahktar, S., *Ash Island Visitor's Book* (2011) p.11

4   Baker, *op. cit.*, p..65

5   Williams, J., 'Molesey Memories', *The Molesey Review*, August/September 1953, p.4

6   East, J.M., 'Karno's Folly', *Theatre Quarterly*, July/September 1971, p.60

7   Baker, *op. cit.*, p.85

8   Baker *op. cit.*, p.80

9   Underhill, M., 'Fred Karno and the Gypsies' Curse', *Country Life*, 17 January 1908, p.152

10 East, *op. cit.*, p.60

11 East, *op. cit.*, p.60

12 Baker, *op. cit.*, p88

13 *The Surrey Comet*, 4 January 1969

14 Baker, *op. cit.*, p.96

9

THE HAMPTON ISLANDS

DIRECTLY ABOVE TAGG'S Island, just off the Hampton Court Road near the ferry crossing lies **Garrick's Ait**.

This fairly small, cigar-shaped island, only accessible by boat, is densely inhabited with twenty-six properties, all built closely together with very small gardens. The island was once known as Church Ait and then Shank's or Shanko's Eyot, until later being named after the famous actor-manager David Garrick. After retiring from the stage, Garrick lived the last twenty-five years of his life in the elegant eighteenth-century Garrick's Villa that stands nearby on the Middlesex bank. He used the island to entertain his guests. Almost directly opposite the island's north bank stands an exquisite little temple that Garrick had built in 1756 to house a bust of William Shakespeare by the famous French sculptor Louis-Francois Roubiliac, which is now in the British Museum. The Grade I listed temple stands in a small, beautifully landscaped garden which is run by a charitable trust. Sadly, Garrick's villa was very badly damaged by fire in October 2008.

The area around the island has obviously been inhabited since ancient times. During dredging at Garrick's Ait in 1970, a flint axe dated around 8300–3700 BC was found making this probably the oldest Neolithic artefact to be found in the Thames. Old eel bucks have also been found on the island, which before Garrick's time was somewhat larger and much lower than it is today. Like many local islands, the level was raised by the dumping of spoil from the Hampton reservoir excavations in 1898–1901. As a result, it became relatively free from flooding, which allowed part of it to be used as an osier bed. It was also heavily wooded and was home to a colony of otters that despite the onset of human habitation and the start of house building, continued to live and breed on the island until the early 1930s.

Prior to the First World War, the island was a popular spot for camping and picnicking and there were no permanent buildings; but later, in the 1920s and 1930s, small plots were rented out. Initially there were tents on the plots, followed by canvas-sided cabins, then wooden cabins. The relatively small size of the plots greatly restricted the size of property that could be erected on the island, so that as late as 1980 Garrick's Ait was still predominantly covered with modest weekend chalets and tents, which have since morphed into solid brick and timber buildings with only a few of the original constructions remaining. In all, however, this little ait presents a cheerful sight bobbing about in the water with its gaily coloured houses.

On the bank opposite the south side of the island is a large area of grassland separating the river from a 1960s housing development built on the site of the old Hurst Park racecourse. Although Garrick's Ait lies nearer to the Surrey bank, its inhabitants almost invariably have to boat across the wider expanse of river to the Middlesex bank for their mainland activities. This makes the islanders more acutely aware of what it actually means to live on an island than those who have merely to cross to their islands via a road or footbridge. For example, in April 2003 a large fire destroyed three bungalows on Garrick's Ait, fortunately with no loss of life. With no bridge, firefighters had to be ferried across on boats belonging to islanders. This illustrates the disadvantages of living on an island that can only be reached by boat. However, the islanders themselves believe that the sense of 'getting completely away, once having set foot on the island', compensates for some real disadvantages.

According to local author Roland Baker, who used to swim here in the 1930s, a tiny islet once stood at the tail of Garrick's Ait. He eloquently describes its sad demise: 'There was not much on the islet, just a little green patch, one solitary tree and mud that oozed through your toes. Over the years, the little island got smaller

Right *Garrick's Temple at Hampton with Garrick's Ait to the left.*

Below *The little eyot off Garrick's Ait before it was dredged away in 1936.*

and smaller, the companionless tree died, and without roots to hold it together the islet rapidly eroded. It was finally dredged away soon after the end of the Second World War.[1]

Rounding the turn in the river from Garrick's Ait lies tiny **Benn's Eyot.** This islet is connected to the Hampton bank by a chain ferry. Almost its entire surface is occupied by the clubhouse of Hampton Sailing Club. The clubhouse, built in 1962, completely dwarfs the island, which takes its name from a local boat building family that owned a boatyard on the Middlesex bank that was demolished in 1947.

The next island is **Platt's Eyot** – and what an island! Due to its dramatic visual impact, Platt's Eyot can justly be referred to as the 'mother' of all Thames islands. This is easily the tallest island in the river and certainly the most impressive, being an important element of views upstream from the Hampton Conservation Area. The eyot sits in an almost central position in the river and is linked to the mainland by an industrial-looking suspension bridge built in 1941, which is primarily a footbridge although small vehicles can pass over it. What is immediately striking about this long baguette-shaped eyot, which Thacker called 'a huge tumulus of an island', are the very steep banks at the upstream end that could almost be described as hilly. Unlike any other Thames island, from the eastern shore you actually have to climb up a steep incline to reach the top of the western part of the eyot. Until the end of the nineteenth century the island was completely flat all over, but from 1898–1901 the then Southwark and Lambeth Water Works Company constructed filter beds on the Hampton side of the river directly opposite the island. All the earth excavated from what was to become the Staines Hill Reservoirs was dumped onto the upper part of the island, thus raising its level to, by Thames island standards, the great height we see today.

Although the island itself is uninhabited, its lower eastern half is occupied by a busy boatyard and light industry workshops with several houseboat moorings. The island is divided into two areas of markedly different character. The eastern end, with its boatsheds, slipways, dry and wet docks and wharfs, is in distinct contrast to the western end, which is a wonderful natural wilderness described by the London Wildlife Trust as 'an interesting mostly undisturbed woodland community in a part of the Borough with few other wildlife habitats.' The island is a particularly important breeding site for song thrushes.

From upstream, the island's high banks are masked by tree foliage, and from downstream the view is dominated by the bulky boatsheds and prow-like pavilion at the eastern end. The steeply wooded boundary conceals the magical interior of the island's western end, where a small winding path meanders off the main track through dense vegetation, until it reaches a dilapidated timber-framed chalet known as Thorneycroft's Cottage. This odd little building was built in 1953, amidst a delightfully secluded garden with a lawn surrounded by shapely oaks, hawthorns and willows on the woodland slopes that fall away to the water's edge. 'In summer the lawn is a haze of red sheep's sorrel flowers, studded with the white and yellow blooms of oxeye daisies and the dancing orange forms of small heath butterflies.'[2]

Up until the late nineteenth century Platt's Eyot was a typical Thames osier bed, and in 1884 Thomas Tagg (of Tagg's Island fame) and Edwin Clark rented the island, where they grew osiers. In 1886 Tagg built a boatyard and a house at the eastern end of the island before moving onto nearby Tagg's Island. According to local historian H.C. Bell, the first recorded industry on the island was an electrical works under the name of J. Johnson in 1889, which used to recharge the batteries of the electric canoes that were popular on the Thames in those days. In 1894 the company was taken over by a German engineer, Moritz Immisch, who designed and built electric launches; the island then became known as Immisch's Island. Its current name probably stems from association with an old Molesey family called Platt, who owned a number of local stores. Around the turn of the century, Chiswick boat builders Thorneycroft's placed orders for small boats to be built by Immisch's yard and in 1908 Thorneycroft's took over from Immisch and established their business on the island.

At the outbreak of the First World War, the Royal Navy's famous coastal motor torpedo boats, the CMBs, were built on the island under utmost secrecy in large sheds specifically constructed for the purpose in 1916. The sheds were timber framed and clad in zinc sheeting painted foliage green for camouflage. One of these is still called the CMB shed today. The CMBs carried just one torpedo which could skim over minefields and attack German destroyers while they were in their home bases. In all, 123 CMBs were built on Platt's Eyot and the Allies were so impressed by their performance that orders came from France, the USA, and later from China, Japan, Siam, Spain, Sweden, Yugoslavia, Holland and Finland.[3] One particular CMB that took part in a daring raid on Russian revolutionaries in Petrograd in 1919, and whose commander, Lieutenant Augustus Agar, was awarded the Victoria Cross, can now be seen at the Imperial War Museum in Duxford, Cambridgeshire.

Interestingly, the Platt's yard also built what is thought to be the first ever aircraft carrier, effectively a barge with winches and water pumps that were towed behind a destroyer with a single Sopworth sea plane on board. The barge would be towed by the destroyer up to a speed of 28 knots: the take-off speed of the Sopworth. The

Platt's Eyot, Hampton, June 2007.

Right Thorneycroft Cottage on Platt's Eyot.

Below The CMB shed on Platt's Eyot.

71

plane would land at sea and then be retrieved by flooding the rear compartment of the barge and then winching the sea plane aboard. This amazing device is now an exhibit in the Fleet Air Arm Museum in Yeovil, Somerset. The pavilion at the eastern end of the island was built as a canteen which was used by the famous Thorneycroft Brass Band for its rehearsals.

Thorneycroft's yard was still operating in the early 1960s, building and repairing boats and providing covered moorings but in 1967 the company moved to Southampton. From then on the yard and the island itself fell into a sorry state of decline, and the old Thorneycroft buildings quietly decayed amidst the encroaching foliage. By the late 1980s the majority of the island's workshops and studio units lay empty and many of the old boatsheds had become abandoned wrecks. In 1990 the island's owners Port Hampton Ltd, an offshoot of the Terrace Hill Group, made an application for the demolition of all buildings on the island and redevelopment for leisure uses, to include luxury apartments and a new road bridge.

This was bound to be a controversial proposal because aside from its unique historical industrial heritage, Platt's Eyot is also significantly important as a natural heritage site. The high western end of the island had already been designated as a Site of Nature Conservation Interest and is included in the Green Belt. With the prospect of the proposed redevelopment of the island, the rest of Platt's Eyot was quickly designated a conservation area in December 1990. This decision was made because of the historical and architectural significance of the island's buildings, its distinctive hilly topography, magnificent trees and splendid wildlife habitats. The boatsheds and features of the Thorneycroft era that dominate the downstream end of the island were granted Grade II listed status the following year. In 1994 *The Independent* described the old boatyard as 'now sufficiently mellow in appearance to be considered part of the island's picturesque confusion rather than an industrial eyesore.'

Following conservation area designation and listing of the boathouses, the controversial redevelopment application was suspended pending the outcome of a public enquiry. In order to preserve the unspoilt wilderness of the island, a pressure group called Campaign Against the Proposed Platt's Eyot Development (Capped) was formed. They wanted to see a heritage, education, training and nature centre on the site. Despite the strong opposition, however, equally controversial plans to build luxury houses and apartments were subsequently resubmitted by the developers. At the time of writing, there appears to be a stalemate with all those involved, including English Heritage, unable to come to an agreement on what would be an acceptable degree of development of the island. More than two decades on from being Grade II listed, the buildings are rapidly deteriorating with one huge old shed now being held together with nothing but ivy. The owners, however, have little incentive to preserve them unless all parties concerned can agree on a plan that will safeguard the island and its heritage.

Meanwhile, the little boatyard area is just about ticking over. Tagg's old house is now used as offices, and together with the industrial buildings, this part of the island has a distinct rustic charm. Worryingly, on the night of Sunday 24 July 2011, a mysterious fire almost completely destroyed one of the old derelict workshops on Platt's. Fire crew and police rushed to the island and managed to evacuate the few people still working there, and police later confirmed that it was a deliberate arson attack. Although there was mention of a few youths seen loitering in the vicinity, one can't help thinking how convenient that yet another historic building on the developer's 'dream island' has been destroyed. Unless something is done soon there will be nothing left of this unique site. It is therefore difficult to predict what the future holds for this incredibly atmospheric island.

Just above Platt's Eyot, where the filter beds are now, there used to be a small island with some ponds on it, which according to Thacker was once called Peggy's Ait, but after 1854 was renamed Pecker's Ait. The Angling Preservation Society was allowed to use ponds at Pecker's Ait for breeding trout. The City of London purchased the island in 1855 and the following year a new channel was opened on its north side, and the space between it and the south bank was filled up. From here the river enters the area of Sunbury-on-Thames.

NOTES

1   Baker, R.G.M., *Thameside Molesey* (London: Barracuda Books Ltd, 1989) p.107

2   *London Ecology Unit Handbook*, No.21, p.9

3   Trimble, N. (ed.) *Life on the Thames Yesterday and Today* (Sunbury and Shepperton Local History Society, 1995) p.22

10

THE SUNBURY ISLANDS

THE STRETCH OF the river between Sunbury and Chertsey is one of the richest areas for bird life in Britain. This is due to the large number of natural ponds, lakes, reservoirs and gravel pits that surround this part of the Thames. As a result all the islands in this area are home to an enormous variety of birds and other wildlife. There are five islands in the Sunbury group, three of them inhabited. The first is **Grand Junction Island**.

Tiny, oval-shaped Grand Junction Island belies its important sounding name, in fact blink and you could miss it, as it lies neatly tucked into a bend of the river opposite Molesey Reservoirs. It is a very private and secluded place, connected to the northern bank by a footbridge that is accessed through a gate to which only islanders have a key. It used to be called Purvis Eyot but takes its present name from the Grand Junction Water Company, which built a water intake on the island to feed the many nearby reservoirs. It is now owned by Thames Water, but the water intake has been redundant for decades. The island is heavily wooded and is a popular spot for pike, perch, bream and roach fishing. There are no permanent dwellings but several timber chalets are used as weekend retreats, reminiscent of the early island pioneer settlements. There are also boat moorings on its southern shore.

The old Metropolitan Water Board used to rent out plots on the island to boat owners, who over the years built small huts on the plots, which were gradually replaced by the chalets we see today. These early settlers also built jetties from which to fish. According to Neil Shimmield, who grew up in Sunbury, two millionaire brothers – Sidney and Samuel Gee – rented the two large central plots from the early 1950s to the mid-1970s. They came down from London at weekends and often entertained their business clients on the island. Today most of the chalets are still owned by the original families. With an idyllic backwater,

dense lush foliage on each side giving welcome shade to those coming off the open river, this charming little island is like a throwback to the early days of Thames island life.

Just moments upstream from Grand Junction Island is a long thin eyot called **Sunbury Court Island**. Private development along this stretch of the Thames has created mass 'bungaloid' growth before the pleasantness of Sunbury village, and Sunbury Court Island is no exception. There isn't an inch of this island, measuring approximately 44 yards by 330 yards (40 by 300 metres) that hasn't been developed. Unlike the other residential islands so far, there is no designated wilderness space or even a small communal garden area. The island is connected to the Middlesex bank by an iron footbridge with an ornate entrance tower that was built to house a sewage pump, although the bridge is not quite as large or as splendid as that of Thames Ditton Island. The island was originally called Hayes Ait but was later named after Sunbury Court, a large house built in 1723 on the riverbank behind it, to which this island and the neighbouring lock island belonged. Sunbury Court was bought by the Salvation Army in 1921 and is still owned by the organisation today. During the long drought of 1976, a stage of ancient eel bucks was uncovered from the mud in the island's backwater.

The majority of the island's twenty-nine modest timber-framed houses are built very close together, leading off a narrow central pathway that runs the length of the island. Despite the slightly claustrophobic nature of the housing, this is a very popular island to live on, as most of the houses have a mainstream as well as a backstream mooring, which offers river access and views from both the front

Sunbury Lock Ait from the Sunbury Bank.

and back gardens. However, the backstream is also densely built up with similar bungalow-type houses, so there is little privacy.

Two famous residents of Sunbury Court Island were *Coronation Street* actor Pat Phoenix and her husband Anthony Booth, father of Cherie Blair. Earlier residents of the large house at the downstream end were actors Ben Lyon and Bebe Daniels, who worked in Hollywood with such stars as Harold Lloyd, Gloria Swanson, Claudette Colbert, Rudolph Valentino and Bing Crosby. Later they became household names as stars of the BBC radio comedy series *Hi, Gang!* from 1940 to 1949 and *Life with the Lyons* from 1951 to 1961. The island, like many on this part of the Thames, used to attract theatrical types because several film studios were located in the vicinity. Now, with many of the studios closed, it has lost its theatrical residents in favour of today's more eclectic mix of inhabitants.

A stone's throw upstream lies **Rivermead Island**. This large, unpopulated island is not easy to identify as an island because just a narrow reed- and rush-filled stream separates it from the mainland, over which a footbridge connects it to the Lower Sunbury bank. Rivermead Island used to be two islands. The downstream end, which 100 years ago was connected to Sunbury Court Island, was known as Swan's Rest, while the upstream one was called Phoenix Island, presumably a reference to the nearby eighteenth-century Phoenix pub. However, they are now completely joined, creating an island of about a quarter of a mile in length.

From the 1950s the island also used to be called 'Swimming Pool Island' as it had a large open-air pool that closed in 1980. This has now been filled in and today Rivermead is basically a small park that at first glance appears to be rather dull; crossing the little bridge, however, you enter a large area of open grassland, and almost immediately your eye is drawn to an enormous plane tree of such magnificent proportions that it must surely be one of the great trees of the Thames. Walking towards the upstream end, the island becomes more wooded, with interesting shrubs and a couple of perfect little sandy beaches.

Since 1877 every second Saturday in August, Sunbury celebrates its Amateur Regatta, one of the last village regattas on the Thames. It is based on Rivermead Island and attracts hoards of visitors. The whole island is decked out in colourful bunting, and stalls, tombolas, coconut shies and jazz bands bring the nostalgic mixture of an old fashioned village fete and traditional Thames boating activities. There is an illuminated sail-past by the Middle Thames Yacht Club and the day ends with a large firework display. In all, this is a very pleasant and tranquil spot for picnics, fishing, swimming and other leisure activities.

Yet another stone's throw brings us to **Sunbury Lock Ait**. This long narrow island lies adjacent to Sunbury Lock and can be reached by crossing a footbridge over the lock cut from the southern bank, as well as by a connection to the lock. The main path, lit by solar lights, runs the length of the ait from the lock to the long footbridge across the weir to the neighbouring island. Before the lock was opened in 1812, the island was known as Sunbury Church Ait, in reference to St Mary's church directly opposite on the Middlesex bank. In Dickens's novel *Oliver Twist*, en route to rob a house in Chertsey, Bill Sykes and Oliver passed the night under an old yew tree in St Mary's churchyard. The island also used to be called Wilson's Eyot after local boat builder George Wilson who had a boatyard on the island.

When the island was chosen in 1811 as the site for the first lock, it was owned by a number of people whose combined interest in the island cost the City of London Corporation a considerable sum of money. According to author John Kemplay, from the time the lock was opened, it caused inconvenience to local people as the old wharf and landing stage near the church were avoided by bargemasters who found it inconvenient to stop because of the siting of the new lock. Instead, they unloaded their merchandise onto the riverbank in front of a private residence, much to the alarm of the owner, who discovered that remonstrating with the bargemen was not a wise course of action.[1] The lock was rebuilt in 1856 with a smaller lock added in 1925.

Although uninhabited now, this has also been an ancient place of human settlement. During the excavations of the lock, a great number of human and animal bones from the late Neolithic and early Bronze Age periods were found. An aerial photograph taken in 1926 shows the island as virtually treeless, in fact it appears as a flat meadow with barrels of hay dotted about, while another taken in 1945 still shows no trees on the Middlesex side of the island, but a sizable group of trees had grown up on the Surrey side. There is a footbridge upstream of the lock, which was once used by horses to tow barges in and out of the old lock, and during the Second World War there were gun emplacements on the island to protect the lock and the nearby reservoirs.

Today, the ait is almost entirely covered by trees and overgrown shrubs, with the occasional strip of rough meadowland along the north bank. Here is the home of the Middle Thames Yacht Club, which is housed in a typically distinctive green timber-framed and zinc-clad building that characterises much of the early Thames island architecture. This is the perfect 'wilderness' island, with little hillocks in the centre surrounded by dense undergrowth criss-crossed with narrow paths.

One can imagine generations of Sunbury children playing swallows and amazons here. These days, it is popular with local dog owners who can let their pets off the leash to run free without the fear of disturbing anyone or anything. The view from Lower Sunbury village across to the island is one of the most scenic on this stretch of the river.

The next island, which is joined to Sunbury Lock Ait by the weir is **Wheatley's Ait**. Unless you are approaching by boat, this sparsely inhabited, traffic-free island must be one of the most difficult islands to get onto, as the footbridge across the Sunbury Lock Ait weir to Wheatley's Ait is actually closed to the public. The only access is by foot via a place on the north side of the island called the Creek, which is a natural waterway whose source is Tumbling Bay, a small weir, constructed in 1934, with several gates at the upstream end of the ait. The Creek then flows between Wheatley's Ait and the mainland for nearly a quarter of a mile, until the Flood Weir, when it becomes straighter and navigable; it then reaches Sunbury Main Weir, where it flows into the Thames.[2]

Getting to the ait has always been difficult. Up until the Second World War, the only access was by boat from the Walton side of the river, and even today some islanders at the extreme west of the island have to boat over from the Walton side. For most of the islanders living west of the then Thames Water Authority (TWA) and now the Environment Agency (EA)'s station, this difficulty was resolved in 1946, when a substantial bridge connecting to the mainland was built across the Creek at the west end of the Creek Estate. Those living on the island east of the TWA were allowed to use the TWA bridge over the Creek.[3]

Wheatley's Ait is also quite confusing to negotiate because, apart from the difficulty of actually getting onto it, the island is in two halves which in turn are divided into three parts. It was once one single island until the spring of 1933 when the building of a new flood channel cut the ait in half. Now the island is in three sections: the downstream end with ten houses, the central section belonging to the EA, and the third part with six houses. The upstream end of the ait is occupied by the chalets of the Thames Camping and Boating Association, one of the oldest camping sites on the river.

Like Sunbury Lock Ait, there are traces of ancient human activity on the island. In June 1907, a 30m long bronze spearhead and a middle Bronze Age rapier were found in the river at Wheatley's Ait, and in 1947 an eleventh-century carpenter's axe was also found on the island. Unusually for a Thames island, Wheatley's Ait appears to have had the same name since the sixteenth century. It formerly belonged to the Manor of Walton Leigh. In a survey of the manor

dating from about 1545, there is a record that a Richard Wheatley had some land near Walton Bridge.[4]

According to Thacker, however, Wheatley's Ait is referred to as 'Scotland Eyte now Wheatley's', but a Mr G.B. Greenwood of the Walton and Weybridge Local History Society suggested that the name Wheatley's Ait appears on the 1866 OS map, and perhaps Scotland sounds like Shotland, which was the old Thames name used for gravel dredged out of the river and dumped – or shot. An indenture dated 24 July 1886, states that Edwin Clark bought 'a piece or parcel of land being part of the eyot commonly known as Wheatley's Eyot' from the family of the late William Hutch.

The island was used as an osier bed until 1895, when it seems that the new tenants were a number of tradesmen who use to meet in a bell tent on Wilson's Eyot (now Sunbury Lock Ait), until the Sunbury villagers complained of their carousing (sound carries loudly across water), and they had to look for a quieter site. And so, in 1897 they bought Wheatley's Ait from the executors of Edwin Clark's will for the sum of £190. The Thames Camping and Boating Association (TCBA) then became their tenants until the TCBA finally bought the upstream part of the island in 1927 for £800 and the Campers formed a limited company.[5] In August 1914 a flying bomb or 'doodlebug' fell on Tumbling Bay destroying the weir, severely damaging several nearby bungalows and killing one man and blinding another.

Idyllic as island life may appear, sometimes, as we have seen with the collapsing bridge on Eel Pie and the hike in ferry fees on Trowlock, islanders can easily find themselves at the mercy of outside forces. In the case of Wheatley's Ait the villain was the Environment Agency (EA), which at the beginning of 2006 held the island's residents hostage after they were banned from using the only safe crossing to the bank. The dispute centred on the road bridge and the footbridge. Traditionally, the ten families on the main eyot paid £60 per year to use them. But the EA, which controls the bridges, demanded that they pay a £7,000 annual toll. The residents eventually agreed to pay £4,000, arguing, not unreasonably, that they could not afford any more. With negotiations stalled, the EA blocked the road bridge with a locked gate and issued solicitor's letters threatening to have anyone using the footbridge prosecuted for trespass. The islanders' only alternative was to paddle or punt across to the mainland: a particularly difficult task for the elderly and risky for all due to the dangerous weir system. The EA also banned deliveries of milk, post, gas and fuel. According to some residents, the EA wanted to get rid of them all so it could sell the valuable land to developers.[6] Eventually, a settlement was reached by which the islanders agreed to pay the agency £700 per household for the access fee and for maintenance of the bridges, but the whole episode proved too much for one elderly lady who apparently died from the stress.

The upstream end of Wheatley's Ait.

Meanwhile, despite its complex geography and access issues, Wheatley's Ait is a very attractive island with some of the friendliest and most contented inhabitants of all the Thames islands. Because the island is sparsely populated, the bungalows on the riverside and creekside have fair-sized gardens interspersed with trees and shrubs and pockets of wilderness. This is definitely the place to live if you like the sound of cascading water, being not only surrounded by the river but also having a weir at either end of the island.

Wheatley's Ait, Sunbury.

On the opposite end of Tumbling Bay is a strip of land that was once, but today is no longer, an actual island, it is called **Beasley's Ait**. Going back to Stone Age times, the earliest river craft on the Thames were dugout canoes, which were merely hollowed-out tree trunks. In October 1966 there was great excitement when one such craft, measuring 18ft, was dug out of the mud at Beasley's Ait. It was dated between the first and second century AD and is now on display in Reading Museum.

NOTES

1   Kemplay, J., *The Thames Locks* (Ronald Crowhurst, 2000) p.30

2   Claxton, W.F., *The Creek, Sunbury on Thames and its Immediate Environment* (Sunbury and Shepperton Local History Society, 1984) p.2

3   Claxton, *op. cit.*, p.10

4   Claxton, *op. cit.*, pp.2–3

5   Claxton, *op. cit.*, p.3

6   *The Evening Standard*, 11 January 2006, p.7, and author's discussion with residents

11

THE SHEPPERTON ISLANDS

THE AREA AROUND Shepperton Lock, the most southerly point of the Thames, contains five islands – four of them inhabited. Like the Sunbury islands, they were first populated by Londoners wanting weekend boltholes away from the grime and smog of the metropolis. Later, during the Second World War, some families, like those on Canvey Island, decided to escape the Blitz by permanently moving onto the islands, where some of their descendents still live. The first of these islands lies on the reach opposite Weybridge and is called **Desborough Island**.

This very large artificially created island covers 45 hectares. It is uninhabited and consists of a patchwork of mainly rough meadowland and playing fields divided by tall hedgerows, giving parts of the island a real 'out in the country' feel. The entire island is ringed with trees and is an important nature conservation site that supports a thriving wildlife population. It can be reached from the Surrey bank by two substantial bridges; the first allows entry to the island, while the second is for exiting it. The southern bank is dead straight as a result of the Desborough Cut, from which the island gets its name. This was dug in the early 1930s to improve the flow of the Thames, and was named after Lord Desborough, a former chairman of the Thames Conservancy, who opened it in 1935. During excavations for the Cut, two small islands, Queensborough Ait and an unnamed islet, were dredged away.

It is the old course of the river, however, that gives this island its special appeal. Here the river meanders around two large loops at the north of the island, and is still as navigable as the Cut but much more lush and scenic. On the south-eastern part of the island is a waterworks and pumping station together with a large reservoir. Next to the waterworks is a sports ground and the north-eastern part of the island is also given over to a large sports field with a wooden clubhouse. Once across the entrance bridge at the south-west corner, the road into the heart of the island is rather desolate and creepy with the metal fencing of the reservoir looming high to your left and the river largely hidden by overgrown shrubs and trees. Aside from this, the island is otherwise a very popular beauty spot and destination for anglers and walkers. There is a footpath alongside the riverbank that encircles the entire island, weaving through the meadowland and small copses, occasionally running to the water's edge, which is indented with enticing little sandy bays and coves. On a hot day this is a pleasant place to swim due to the soft sandy riverbed off the shore, which is free from weeds and other obstructions.

Although it is actually owned by the North Surrey Water Company, Universal Vandals Rugby Club, the Environment Agency, Surrey County and Elmbridge Borough Council, the island is managed by Elmbridge's commons management team. Recently efforts have been made to enhance the environment of the island with new hedges being laid to improve wildlife habitats. This is a unique area of wild riverside meadows; some may say a bit too wild as a hilly part of the downstream end becomes less respectable after dusk. Desborough Island is an odd place in many ways, where people seem to walk around eight to ten dogs at any one time, which can be a bit disconcerting as most are off the lead and get very excited at the sight of the river. There are further plans to improve the island, not only for wildlife but also for humans by making it more family friendly with a riverside nature trail, wider paths, more lighting and a picnic area. Perhaps though, the island is just too large to give the visitor that sense of security and intimacy that is such a precious feature of smaller islands.

Eyot House on D'Oyly Carte Island, Shepperton.

Continuing upriver, the next island near Shepperton Lock and the River Wey confluence is **D'Oyly Carte Island.**

This oval-shaped little Island is approached from the Weybridge bank via an ornate arched metal bridge built in 1964 to provide access to the island's only house. Prior to that, the island was reached by a cumbersome, hand operated chain ferry that was summoned by ringing a bell on the towpath. D'Oyly Carte Island was originally a mere sandbank in the Thames that was raised to its present height as a result of dredging gravel. This island provides a good example of how frequent were the name changes of many Thames islands. According to Thacker the channel between the island and the left bank of the Thames was known as Silly Cut and in 1885 he found a reference to a Silly Eyot at this point. The island has always been a haven for nesting swans, and Thacker also found references to the island as Swan Ait, and before that in 1794 as Folly Ait. Later it was simply called The Eyot, and was popular with anglers fishing for perch, pike and chub.

The island has just one large house, Eyot House, which was built in 1888 by the opera impresario Richard D'Oyly Carte (1844–1901), who also built the Savoy

Theatre – the first in London to have electric lights – to produce and perform the Gilbert and Sullivan Savoy Operas. In 1887 D'Oyly Carte was boating on the Thames with his sons when he saw the island, which he later bought and built what was then a very grand house with a footbridge. His family used the island as their country retreat where they allegedly kept a pet crocodile. The building has since been refurbished, converted into flats and then converted back into a private house. The island was often used for rehearsals by the D'Oyly Carte Savoy Opera Company, and in 1894 a local journalist heard the rehearsals as he passed by the island on a boat. The next day he wrote in the *Surrey Gazette*: 'No doubt we shall soon get used to calling the island "D'Oyly Carte Island" instead of The Eyot.'[1]

Eyot House appears disproportionately large for the size of the island. From the front it is quite an attractive building being built in the Arts and Crafts style. It is approached directly from the bridge or from steps up from the river bank. Its white-painted façade, framed by trees and shrubs, is enhanced by a wooden balcony surrounding the whole house. Towards the western end of the island the wilderness clears into a small garden with a rustic loggia. The island offers moorings to small boats around most of the island.

In a 1995 article entitled 'A Little Bit of Paradise', Andria Phoku, who bought Eyot House in 1988, says that when she and her husband were first given the keys to Eyot House by its then owner Commander Hardy, she could see tears in the eighty-two-year-old gentleman's eyes. She went on to describe how the island was used as a location by film companies:

> One was particularly interesting not only for ourselves, but for the many locals who came to watch the activities from the towpath. It took the film makers two weeks to clad the metal bridge to the island with wood. This was to make it look like the 1940s. Parts of the house were dressed to look like a German aristocrat's country residence outside Berlin. The following week we had *Alias Smith and Jones* filming for a day and had to put up with caged 'bodies' all over the place. Smith and Jones were doing a great take off of *Apocalypse Now* which starred Martin Sheen and Marlon Brando.[2]

Leaving D'Oyly Carte Island we come almost immediately to **Lock Island**. It is from this small island that the very busy Shepperton Lock is operated. Most of this half-moon-shaped Island has remained a dense undisturbed wilderness with some exceptionally high trees and plenty of wildlife, including water voles and other aquatic mammals. The first lock was opened in 1813 and a house for the keeper was built with a small relief channel behind the lock house. Prior to this it was called Sawbridge Island. According to Thacker, in 1814 Lord Portmore complained to the City that, since the new lock cut was made, his tenant of the 'meadow called Stadbury had no way to carry off his hay.' This appears to indicate that the lock island was previously joined to the Middlesex bank, and became an island only when the waters broke through Stoner's Cut, the channel to the north of the island that today is the main channel.

The island's Lock House was destroyed by a German bomb on 29 September 1940, which demolished it and killed the lock keeper's daughter. The keeper now lives in the older property at the eastern end of the island, previously the area engineer's residence. The Thames River Police also have a station on the island. Today the waters by Lock Island are used for white water and slalom canoeing. Coloured poles, suspended from overhead wires, mark out the slalom course, which is used for training purposes and competitive events. The British Olympic team has trained here.[3] The area surrounding the lock itself is nicely maintained with a large lawn and flowerbeds. There is a small café with welcoming chairs and tables where visitors can sit and watch the antics at the lock. This area is beloved of the weekend boating fraternity who aimlessly ply their huge white gin palaces up and down this stretch of the river, causing major congestion at the lock and endless amusement for onlookers.

A pretty cottage on Hamhaugh Island, Shepperton.

At the side of the Lock Island café is a tree-lined path that leads to a magnificent weir, across which runs a narrow walkway to **Hamhaugh Island**.

This relatively large, bell-shaped island has two large dramatic weirs on its northern perimeter. Here the tight river bends and shallows between Weybridge and Walton made river travel dangerous. To solve the problem, Shepperton Lock and Weir were built across the top of one bend, so creating Hamhaugh Island. This is a well-populated, traffic-free island that must surely vie, along with Wheatley's Ait, as one of the most difficult of all the inhabited Thames islands to gain access to. Arriving by boat may be fairly straightforward, but access by foot is difficult, as you have firstly to cross over the gates at Shepperton Lock and then walk down a narrow path enclosed by trees on both sides, then walk across the weir, and finally down another lonely, heavily wooded path until you reach a large ornate metal gate. This opens onto the island's main path which runs past a large triangular grassy space dotted with trees in the centre of the island. Walking onto this island from the weir is a distinctly unique experience and a little scary if you are arriving after dark or at a time when there are few other people around.

At the end of the nineteenth century summer camping started to become a popular activity and like many other Thames islands, Hamhaugh became a favoured summer campsite for Londoners. In 1900 the island belonged to George Dunton (1837–1915), a local boat builder, who rented out plots for tents to be erected during the summer months. Unfortunately, Mr Dunton drowned in the Thames in March 1915, while waiting for his son Jack to ferry him back to Shepperton after a night out in Weybridge. He is buried in St Nicholas churchyard. Following his father's death, his son decided to give regular campers the option of buying their own plots, which most people did. The occupiers quickly replaced the tents with crude sheds and later timber chalets and bungalows.

Before the construction of Shepperton Lock created Hamhaugh Island, this bend in the river was known as Stadbury Meadows and the island was primarily used for hay making rather than osier cultivation. Until the beginning of the 1930s a large horse ferry was moored near Ferry Lane, which would take horses and wagons over to the island during the haymaking season. The island had an abundance of fruit trees at that time: apples, pears, peaches and several varieties of plum. In 1995 a fascinating booklet called 'Shepperton's Island Dwellers', was published by Sunbury and Shepperton Local History Society. Not only does it give a valuable insight into early life on Hamhaugh Island, but the stories told must surely mirror the early days of most of the inhabited Thames islands, and thus this booklet provides a unique record of a brief but important moment in Thames island history. The following paragraphs are accounts of early life on Hamhaugh, parts of which are quoted from this wonderful booklet.

One of the island's original occupants, Winifred Scholfield, tells of how, from 1900, her mother's family camped at Hamhaugh during August, after the hay was mown. On the first occasion they came in a horse-drawn van containing tents, bedding, a stove and provisions from Chelsea. The van was parked at Dunton's boatyard and the horse taken back to Chelsea. She describes how her grandmother and the children camped throughout August, the 'working' members of the family came just at weekends; they travelled by the 10.17p.m. train from Waterloo to Shepperton and walked to the lock where Mr Kirby, the lock keeper, would unlock the gate of the lower weir for them. By the 1920s the menfolk of some camping families would travel daily to their work from Shepperton station in the mornings to avoid crossing the river, but in the evenings they came to Weybridge station because there was a better rail service there. Little buses ran from the station to Weybridge Rowing Club, from where the men gave distinctive calls to their wives to come and fetch them in boats.[4]

Two 'Founding Families' of Hamhaugh Island were the Gentry and Scholfield families. In 1920 Mr Gentry and Mr Scholfield formed the Hamhaugh Islander's Association; the first aim of the association was to buy the triangle of land in the centre of the island and maintain it as a perpetual open space and so prevent it becoming a 'warren' in the hands of speculators.[5] By the late 1920s a few campers had built wooden bungalows while several were First World War Nissen huts. Those who purchased plots gave them bizarre names such as Whyworrie, Weyknot and Watabahtit. There was a toilet in the middle of the Green – a flag was hoisted when it was in use! Drinking water was collected from Harris's boatyard on the Weybridge side of the river, now Tappin's boatyard. This water was kept strictly for drinking and cooking, water for washing up and washing oneself was from the river.[6]

The first proper chalet on the island was erected in the late 1920s and during the next twenty years the dwellings became larger and more elaborate, usually by separate additions to the original shack. Tents continued to be used by two households until 1938. Until 1919 there were communal latrine sheds with buckets; by then most people had installed private lavatories. People burned most of their rubbish; at a later date bins could be kept on Lock Island that were emptied by the local authority. Mains water did not reach the island until 1959 when three stand pipes were erected; a communal pump for drinking water was sunk on the Green in the 1940s, but before that mains water had to be fetched from taps on

the mainland. Electricity was installed in 1948; before that paraffin lamps were used for lighting and primus stoves for cooking. In 1994 gas was piped over the river as many people wanted gas central heating.[7] This rustic life was apparently very appealing as one 'pioneer' Winifred Schofield reminisced: 'There was great satisfaction in the simple life of early times on the island. Until the 1920s the river was very quiet – deserted in mid-week, and although we were close to civilisation, there was a feeling of remoteness and living an ideal life.'[8]

The first household to stay the year round did so in 1928 and by the late 1930s, there were a few families living on the island all year round, including Gert and Horsey Brion who lived in 'Sans Souci'. They kept a small shop in a shed on their plot for the convenience of weekenders and holiday folk. If islanders heard on the grapevine that someone was ill or had suffered an accident, they were there on the doorstep with first aid kits and kind offers of help: there was a great spirit of comradeship.[9] An air raid shelter was built on the Green at the beginning of the war. Air raid wardens were very strict about blackout as the river was used as a route finder. Some campers moved onto the island permanently to escape the worst of the Blitz. In 1951 George and Edna Gratton moved onto Hamhaugh and became the first family to have children on the island. As Edna explains: 'We were not very popular with some older residents who preferred the island to be a quiet haven for adults. Our son born in 1957 was the first island baby, after a few years other young families arrived. At first we had large canisters with special filters for purifying river water. When mains water was brought to three standpipes on the island we had two 30 gallon tanks on the roof which we filled once a week.'[10]

The island continued to grow in popularity. Well known former residents include *The Good Life* actor Felicity Kendall and Bob Mackenzie of election 'swingometer' fame. Today islanders give an annual payment to the Hamhaugh Island Residents' Association which covers the cost of insurance, weir passes, maintenance of firefighting equipment and upkeep of the central Green with its huge copper beech tree, where residents hold their many social events. Nowadays, Hamhaugh Island's forty-six houses are a far cry from the original settlers' timber chalets. Many have been rebuilt in brick and some command extremely high prices: at the time of writing there is one house for sale for nearly £1,000,000! A price some are willing to pay to live the island dream.

Back in the main body of the river above Shepperton Lock is the exotically named **Pharaoh's Island.**

This very attractive pear-shaped island is traffic free and accessed only by boat. It has twenty-three homes, many with Egyptian-inspired names such as Philae,

Pharaoh's Island, Shepperton.

A fine copper beech on Pharaoh's Island, Shepperton.

Luxore, Memphis and The Sphinx. This is because the island was reputedly presented to Admiral Nelson in 1798, in recognition of his victory at the battle of the Nile. Apparently Nelson was known to have enjoyed fishing in the area and used the island as a fishing retreat. Before this historic naval victory, Pharaoh's Island used to be much larger and was used for osier growing.

In 1871 the Thames Conservancy ordered the planting of willows, poplars and alders at Pharaoh's. This was done in order to improve the aesthetic view of the river, and has more than achieved its objective, for today these trees still stand and are among the finest on any of the islands. Once on the island, there is a central pathway leading to a large green used for various events in the island's social calendar. There is a good sense of space on this island as the houses all have decent-sized front and rear gardens, and are spread around the island's perimeter thus avoiding the claustrophobic atmosphere of some other inhabited islands.

Until the 1980s Pharoah's Island was very different from the exclusive riverside residence it has become today. At that time, apart from two large brick-built houses with lawned gardens, the other dwellings were just a motley collection of ramshackle wooden bungalows, most of them with verandas. According to one resident who moved to Pharoah's Island in April 1941, the island had no water laid on so people had to row to the ferry point on the tow path to get drinking water, while pumping in river water for all other uses. The island had no main drainage until the 1960s and all the bungalows had cess pits. In 1941 only about half the bungalows were lived in, the rest were still regarded as holiday homes.[11] Past residents include the actor Ian Hendry, who starred in the film *Get Carter* and was the original star of *The Avengers* before Patrick McKnee.

Pharaoh's has a very relaxed and peaceful atmosphere about it, and for a well-developed island it has an abundance of wildlife. On a really sad note, in January 2011, island resident Keith Lowde, sixty-six, drowned along with a friend, Rex Walford, seventy-six, when their boat capsized in freezing water as Mr Lowde was rowing his companions across the short channel to the mainland. Melting snow had caused havoc in the waters around Shepperton that Christmas and New Year, and this was a cruel reminder of the challenges and dangers that face island dwellers with boat-only access to their homes.

A little way upstream of Pharaoh's Island on the left bank the area known as Dockett Eddy used to be an island called Dock Eyot, later corrupted to Dog Ait. Thacker noted in 1919 that scarcely anyone remembered that it had once been an island, nor was it even recognisable as one.

The title itself survives in Dockett Point and Dockett Eddy House.

NOTES

1   *The Surrey Gazette*, 18 June 1894

2   Phoku, A., and Brooking, V (ed.), *Shepperton's Island Dwellers* (London: Sunbury and Shepperton Local History Society, June 1995) pp.42–3

3   Trimble, N. (ed.), *Life on the Thames Yesterday and Today* (Sunbury and Shepperton Local History Society, 1995) p.78

4   Scholfield, W., 'Hamhaugh Pioneers 1900–1959' in Brooking, *Shepperton's Island Dwellers* (Lonon: Sunbury and Shepperton Local History Society, June 1995) pp.9–10

5   Hadlow, S., 'Founding Families', in Brooking, *op. cit.*, p.8

6   Noble, J., 'Hamhaugh Island – The Early Years', in Brooking, *op. cit.*, pp.28–9

7   Scholfield, *op. cit.* p.11

8   *Ibid.*, p.14

9   Clifton, G., 'Life on Hamhaugh Island 58 years ago (1937)', in Brooking, *op. cit.*, pp.22–3

10 Gratton, G. and Gratton, E., 'Recollections', in Brooking, *op. cit.*, p.32

11 Chivers, P., 'Fifty Years on Pharoah's Island', in Brooking, *op. cit.*, p.3

12

THE STAINES ISLANDS

THIS STRETCH OF the river around Staines has a gloomy past. According to Henry Taunt, popular legend told that in the mid-seventeenth century, when highwaymen terrorised the main London road from Hounslow Heath to Colnbrook, and Claude du Val (1643–70) headed the band, the bodies of all travellers who lost their lives in the frequent deadly encounters were brought here by night in heavily weighted sacks and thrown into the Thames. Claude du Val came from France and though a notorious highwayman is also remembered for his eccentric desire to teach English footpads to rob politely. He was hanged at Tyburn Gallows aged just twenty-seven.[1] That said, the Staines islands are far from gloomy. There are nine islands in this group, four of them inhabited. The first of these islands occurs on a naturally formed and impressive oxbow bend in the river and is called **Penton Hook Island**.

This large, uninhabited and traffic-free island is immensely attractive, hanging like a pear-shaped earring from the adjacent Penton Hook Lock. It was artificially created by a navigation channel when the tight meander of the river was bypassed by the construction of Penton Hook Lock Cut in 1815. Prior to this, the strip of land around which the river wound was only 50 yards across, and Thames waters would often flood across the neck of the 'hook'. In fact, the neck was flooded so often that bargemen began using it as a short cut leading to the construction of the lock. Before 1815, the island was used for the cultivation of hay. Getting onto the island involves walking over the sluice gates from little **Penton Hook Lock Island** onto another tiny islet, then crossing onto Penton Hook Island itself. The lock island is half-moon shaped with a tiny keepers' hut and pleasant gardens. During the summer of 2011 the Thames Anglers' Conservancy carried out work on the island to improve habitats for wildlife and breeding fish. A fish bypass channel was created on the island, which provides valuable gravels for

fish spawning. Logs were also piled together to create refuges for invertebrates and small animals.

Penton Hook Island was once a burial ground during the Great Plague of 1665, and nowadays it is managed by the Environment Agency as a terrific nature reserve. It is home to herons, large colonies of parakeets, kingfishers, grebes and water voles and has its own fish spawning channel, which was constructed in 1999. The island, which is very popular with anglers, is interspersed with a range of meandering paths criss-crossing through forest, meadows and little grassy clearings dotted with the occasional picnic table. This wonderfully secluded piece of natural woodland is stunningly beautiful because its western bank lies opposite an equally wild wooded peninsula and the channel between the two, capped by the tumbling bay weir, is almost Amazonian in parts.

A short hop upstream from Penton Hook is **Truss's Island**. This tiny uninhabited island is situated just off the Surrey bank, almost halfway between Chertsey and Egham. Just over 100 yards long, it is separated from the mainland by a small channel, across which are two little wooden bridges. There are some splendid trees on the island as well as several pollarded willows, evidence of the island's earlier use as an osier bed. Although the surroundings are a bit dull and suburban, this is a rewarding little island to visit. Named after Charles Truss, one of the most influential people associated with the Thames, the islet has been thoughtfully landscaped to resemble a miniature riverside park.

Charles Truss was appointed clerk of works to the Worshipful Committee of Thames Navigation of the City of London in 1774. His task was to further develop

Truss's Island, Egham.

Interior of Truss's Island, Egham.

the navigability of the river by improving the locks and towpaths. The name of Truss's Island commemorates an important episode in the history of the Thames. The amount of commercial traffic using the river increased enormously during the eighteenth century but, as a consequence, concern developed regarding its deficiencies as a means of transport, particularly for barges. These defects included crude and inadequate locks, discontinuous towpaths and complete uncertainty as to whether there was sufficient depth to allow barges to navigate the river.

The City had almost been deprived by parliament of its immemorial right to control the lower Thames highway because of its earlier failures, and it was now determined that it would safeguard its right by positive action. This was certainly needed, for as Truss reported in 1775, the obstructions were numerous 'and much increased by the last extraordinary flood: the banks of the river have been washed

away in many places and new shoals raised by that flood, so that the barges are laid aground in places where they used to meet with no obstruction. The towing paths in various places are becoming intolerable and in several parts quite taken away.' For thirty-six years Truss pursued his task with such zeal that by the time of his retirement in 1810, the lower Thames was fully navigable and a grateful City Corporation awarded him a pension of £200 a year.

Thacker mentions an interesting reference to this island:

In a letter dated 10 June 1827, a General Scott wrote to a Mr Leach (the City navigation clerk of works) saying that in the course of rowing about the previous week he discovered an uninhabited island near Savory's Weir, which from an inscription on a column erected there, proves that the island has been visited some years ago, and it is called Truss's Island. This property is coveted by him, firstly because it might fall into the hands of some troublesome neighbour, and secondly the ladies of his family might find some amusement upon landing on this island and planting it with Shrubs. General Scott would be glad of a lease.' The column was 'a mark-stone with the City's arms engraved, and the general, whom it appears was granted a lease, was forbidden to remove it.'[2]

General Scott eventually bought the island and the ladies of his household did indeed plant some shrubs, the remnants of which can still be seen today.

In the decades after Scott's death, however, the island became increasingly neglected and heavily overgrown, so much so that by the end of the nineteenth century it could no longer be called a true island as the northern end of the small channel separating it from the mainland had silted up. By 1950 the whole of the channel had silted up so that the island practically joined the Surrey bank. The island continued to deteriorate until Runnymede Borough Council eventually took control of it in 1991. The following year a major restoration programme began, which included digging out the overgrown channel and making it a true island once more.

The revival of Truss's Island is remarkable. It is now a welcoming and enjoyable place to relax and watch the antics of the large group of swans and ducks that have made the island their home. There are a number of facilities, including a public slipway, a riverside path, fishing platforms for the disabled, a picnic area, benches at every vantage point, a temporary mooring and wildlife feeding steps. As if this wasn't enough for such a small island, two large pictorial signs give a thorough explanation of the island's history, as well as displaying ancient artefacts discovered in the nearby riverbed. At the foot of the upstream end is an ornate sign dedicated to 'The Conservators of the River Thames', and at the very centre of the island stands a beautifully restored inscribed stone, the 'column' mentioned by General Scott, erected in 1804 by the City Corporation, to commemorate the work of Charles Truss. In fact the whole of this little island is a fitting memorial to one of the most important men associated with the River Thames.

Passing under Staines Bridge on the right-hand bank is **Church Island**. This triangular-shaped, medium-sized island nestles snugly in the bend opposite Ashby Lammas recreation ground. It is very attractive, traffic-free and well wooded with around half a dozen or so houses discretely hidden among the dense canopy of trees. This island used to be reached from the mainland by an old chain ferry, but today it is connected by a footbridge to the Thames Path and old Staines village,

which in marked contrast to modern Staines, is very picturesque, clustered around the large church of St Mary's from which the island gets its name.

Just behind Church Island on the north bank of the river once stood an ancient landmark called the London Stone, which from 1285 marked the upper limit of the jurisdiction of the City of London over the River Thames. On the top of the original stone the inscription: 'God preserve the City of London', AD 1280.' is still legible today. The stone we see on the riverbank today is actually a replica that was placed here in 1986. In order to preserve it, the original is currently housed in the Spelthorne Museum in Staines.

Continuing along the bank of Ashby Lammas Park is the highly illusive **Hollyhock Island**. This island is very hard to distinguish on a map and equally difficult to locate on the ground, as its foliage has obscured the little ditch that separates it from the park. Unfortunately, it is also virtually impossible to define from the river. I don't believe this is now a true island, so moving on just a few yards brings us to **Holm Island**.

This long, thin island is easily recognisable as an island and is connected to the mainland by a metal footbridge. Its silted backwater was the main barge channel in the eighteenth century. It is an unusual island because the trees, along with shrubs and wild roses, are dotted among the grassland, resembling an orchard. Situated almost in the centre of the island is a large, vacuous-looking 1970s-style house called The Nest, which is built on stilts. This replaced an earlier property where, during the 1930s, King Edward VIII (later the Duke of Windsor) courted Mrs Wallis Simpson. Altogether this is a very pretty, albeit slightly mysterious island.

Shortly after Bell Weir Lock on the reach near Hythe End lies **The Island**. A relatively small inhabited island, it is connected to the Berkshire side of the river by a single bridge, which spans a narrow channel of the Thames. It is an unusual shape: wide at the upper end tapering off into a thin tail. Although it is heavily developed with around twenty properties built quite closely together, there is a welcoming, contented feel to this island. A little pathway runs the length of the island facing the small inner channel, which is lined with trees and wild flowers and has the look of a country lane. Despite not having any noticeable communal open space like many other inhabited islands, this is a very agreeable place indeed, with one inhabitant describing life there as 'being on permanent holiday'.

The picturesque inner channel at The Island, Hythe End.

The Island, Hythe End.

Rounding a sharp loop in the river is another illusive but very famous island called **Magna Carta Island**. This uninhabited island is long and thin, around 3 acres in size and heavily wooded. It is quite difficult to reach from the mainland as the path to it crosses a very wild and remote series of fields. It is not easy to distinguish from the water either as the tiny channel separating it from the bank is heavily overgrown. The island is in fact an extension of the water meadows of Runnymede, alongside which stands an ancient yew tree reputed to be over 2,000 years old. The island once belonged to the twelfth-century nunnery of Ankerwyke Priory and today its wooded banks conceal its ruined, ivy-clad remains. Brindley's map of 1770 shows that a barge channel once lay between Magna Carta Island and a much smaller island that still existed on a map of 1823. In 1813 the island was covered in willows, which shaded a fisherman's hut that was later rebuilt as an ornate Gothic cottage.

A number of romantic myths have evolved around several Thames eyots, and Magna Carta Island is one of them, for it is supposedly upon this island that King John was compelled by the barons to sign the Magna Carta on 15 June 1215. This document granted 'liberties to all free men of our kingdom', thereby establishing the principles of freedom guaranteed by law, which today forms the basis of individual rights in English law. No one knows exactly where the actual Charta was sealed. The location given in the Charta itself is 'between Staines and Windsor in the meadow which is called "Runimed"'. Later chroniclers, however, altered the phrase to 'an island between Staines and Windsor', and so gave rise to the myth of Magna Carta Island.

The erroneous tradition was begun by the lord of a Buckinghamshire manor, George Simon Harcourt, who built the Gothic cottage on the island in 1834 and installed a stone slab there called the Charta Stone that was inscribed with the words: 'Be it remembered that on this island, 15 June 1215, John King of England signed Magna Carta; and in the year 1834, this building was erected in commemoration of that great and important event, by George Simon Harcourt, Lord of this Manor and then High Sheriff of this County.' One can only assume that Mr Harcourt was determined to be associated with this notable event by claiming that it took place on his land.

Whatever the truth is about this island, it will forever be associated with the famous Charta. If the Charta was not actually sealed on the island, then it did at least provide the backdrop to one of the most important chapters in English history. As Jerome K. Jerome wrote in 1889: 'Slowly the Baron's bright-decked barges leave the shore of Runnymede. Slowly against the swift current they work their ponderous way, till they grate against the bank of the little island that from this day will bare the name of Magna Charta Island. And King John has stepped upon the shore…and the great cornerstone in England's temple of liberty has … been firmly laid.[3]

A short distance upstream is **Pat's Croft Eyot**. This is a small, narrow, privately owned island which is very heavily wooded. It is attached to the Wraysbury bank by a little wooden footbridge over a wide inner channel. The eyot used to be called Sanderson's Ait and was later known alternatively as Bucks Ait or Ankerwyke Ait because it used to belong to the Ankerwyke Priory estate, which had a large fishery and eel bucks here. Today it has one house in the centre with various craft moored alongside the outer bank. For some reason its tree cover gives it a rather dishevelled and scruffy appearance.

The river now rounds a bend into Old Windsor from where there is the largest collection of islands through to Windsor town.

NOTES

1   Read, S. (ed.), *The Thames of Henry Taunt* (Sutton Publishing, 1989) p.166
2   Thacker, F.S., *The Thames Highway Vol.2: Locks and Weirs* (David & Charles, 1968 (first published London, 1920)) pp.396–7
3   Jerome, J.K., *Three Men in a Boat* (J.W. Arrowsmith, 1889) p.180

13

THE WINDSOR ISLANDS

THERE ARE SIXTEEN islands in this group of which only five are inhabited. Just up from the Bells of Ouzeley pub in Old Windsor is a very small island that is usually unnamed on Thames maps. At one time it was called Heron Eyot and now it is known as **Kingfisher Island**.

This tiny eyot is tucked neatly into the Wraysbury bank from which it is separated by a very narrow but picturesque channel. There are just three houses on the island, which is connected to the mainland by a very rustic-looking footbridge built by the owner of the house at the downstream end. He bought it in the 1970s from the wife of a former mayor of London. Apparently she was a well-travelled woman and stocked her garden with some strange exotic plants and trees, which today provide a wonderful display at the island's tip.

A short distance upstream sits **Friary Island**. This inhabited island can just about be called an island, as it is connected to the Wraysbury bank by a small road bridge across an almost dry, reed-filled ditch that suggests it might hold water during periods of heavy rainfall. The island lies just across the river from Old Windsor, where there was once a Friary from which the island took its name. From the river the island looks pleasing enough with gardens fronting the water's edge but from the one road running the island's length, you are transported into pure suburbia with no sense of being on a Thames island. There are around forty properties lining the road with very few of the original timber-framed chalets remaining, all the rest having been rebuilt on relatively small plots, giving an overall claustrophobic feel. In general, the large, modern suburban-looking houses have been built in a rather garish and obtrusive manner, giving the island a somewhat sterile feel and robbing it of atmosphere.

Moving quickly on we come to a tiny eyot known as **Friday Island**. This miniscule patch of woodland sits on the right of the river just below Old Windsor Lock. Apparently, this tiny islet got its name because it resembles Man Friday's footprint, but having been all round the island, I fail to see any footprint shape. It is just a perfectly formed little oblong ait, a real treat to behold. In fact, with its willows shrouding the entire islet and sweeping the water's edge, it resembles Dougal from *The Magic Roundabout*. It contains just one small cottage, which sports a brand new thatched roof and is almost completely concealed by a large weeping willow. The cottage windows peep seductively through the foliage of its secretive garden. From 1966 until his death in 1991, this was the home of Dr Julius Grant, the famous forensic scientist and intelligence officer, who proved in 1984 that the infamous *Hitler Diaries*, published with great fanfare in *The Sunday Times*, were in fact a forgery. The lock keeper recalled Dr Grant saying that whenever he rowed his little punt onto the island, he felt it was like going a million miles away. The present owners just use the little isle as a weekend retreat.

Directly above Friday Island is **Old Windsor Lock Island**. This small oval-shaped island is joined to the Old Windsor bank by the lock that was built in 1822. The northern half of the island is devoted to the workings of the lock and the keeper's cottage with its pleasant garden. On the other side of the island is a small weir,

Friday Island, Old Windsor.

There are thirty-seven houses situated entirely in the southern part of the island in an avenue of modest bungalows, some of which are set back from the water and sunk behind a high bank that totally obscures their view of the river. There are, however, some larger and more expensive dwellings in the upstream corner facing the weir. On first impressions Ham Island does not look that appealing as the cut itself is rather claustrophobic. Nevertheless, although the old river course is unnavigable because it is blocked by the weir, if you are travelling by boat and don't mind turning round again, the journey around the island is very pleasant, with mainly rural surroundings on the mainland bank.

A few yards beyond the big weir is another tiny eyot called **Lion Island**. This very picturesque uninhabited islet, around 50 yards long, is owned by the Crown Estate. Despite regularly flooding, it is thickly wooded with an enchanting and secluded backwater flanking the northern bank. It is unclear how Lion Island got its name but it is a remnant of three parallel islands that existed at this point before the creation of the New Lock Cut that formed Ham Island. One of these was called Nickcroft Ait, and an ancient eel buck setting known as 'Newman's Bucks' existed between two of them.

Continuing on up to Dachet we come to **Sumptermead Ait**. This uninhabited island is almost impossible to determine on a map, given that it is merely a thin wooded strip separated by a very narrow channel on the Datchet side just after Victoria Bridge. Off the river, it is equally hard to find because it originally had just the thinnest of back channels linking it to the Datchet bank, which has now almost totally dried up. In 1995 a new riverside path was created here for the diverted Thames path. The island is named after the great meadow behind it, which is now a golf course.

Sumptermead Meadow was owned by the Priory of St Helen of Bishopsgate as early as 1263. At the dissolution of the monasteries in 1540, all of St Helen's endowments were seized by Henry VIII and sold for profit. The meadow and the ait changed hands several times over the course of the centuries, until the land was bought by the Crown Estate in 1875 in order to protect the riverbank from development. It was subsequently leased to Datchet Golf Club.

constructed in 1836 and connecting it to the next island. The rest of the island is given over to sparse woodland with moorings on the eastern bank.

Adjacent to the little weir on the right of the lock island is the tip of **Ham Island**. This is one of the largest islands in the Thames and was created when the course of the river was diverted in 1822 via a cut to provide a more navigable route to Old Windsor. Because of its great size, Ham doesn't actually feel like an island even though you have to cross a rather shabby metal road bridge to get onto it. This sparsely inhabited island is almost square in shape with the main road running through to the centre where there is a large sewage treatment works that was constructed in the 1870s. The main body of the island is comprised of open fields and unkempt scrubland, but its perimeter is ringed with a diverse cover of trees.

Black Pott's Ait, Datchet.

As the river approaches Windsor we come across **Black Pott's Ait**. This relatively large uninhabited island is around 150 yards long and the southern end lies just under Black Pott's Railway Bridge. It is completely wild. In fact, there are no paths whatsoever and it is so thickly wooded and knee high with stinging nettles and brambles, that it is virtually impenetrable. It doesn't look as if anyone has set foot on this mysterious island for decades. It is the only Thames island I have been on where I have actually lost my way. It has four tiny little islet clumps at its northern tip that appear to have once been surrounded by a sort of wooden staked fence. This could possibly be the remains of an old fishing weir, which as late as 1868 ran straight upstream from the head of this island, leaving only a narrow opening round the end of the next island. The island was famous for its eel traps, the remnants of which can also still be seen close to the bridge.

Almost immediately after leaving Black Pott's comes **Romney Eyot**. This is in fact two very long, thin islands separated by the small tumbling bay weir at Toll's Hole, built in 1903; the first island is joined to Romney lock, which was first built in 1797. From time immemorial these uninhabited islands have been joined by some form of bridge, and are often collectively referred to as 'The Romneys'. Both islands consist of sparse tree cover interspersed with patches of grass and scrubland. It has always been a popular place for angling. Isaak Walton, the author of the *The Compleat Angler* used to fish from Romney Eyot.

At the tip of Romney Lock Island, a spit of land known as 'The Cobbler' divides the weir stream from the lock cut. At the end of the eighteenth century, The Cobbler, which was used by horses towing barges, was extended to within 40 yards of Windsor Bridge for the purpose of diverting the flow of water into the nearby Tangier Mill Stream. In the 1840s there were plans developed to build a railway line along Romney Eyot, which was then owned by the Commissioners of the Thames Navigation. In order to stop this public intrusion and pollution so close to Eton College, the school bought the island from them. So the railway went to neighbouring Black Pott's Ait instead. On 4 June each year Eton College celebrates the memory of King George III for his financial generosity towards the school, throwing a huge fireworks display that takes place on Romney Eyot.

In a bid apparently to reduce the carbon footprint of the royal family, in September 2011 two giant Archimedes screws were lowered into place at Romney Weir, in order to provide Windsor Castle with hydroelectric power. Alongside the screws is a £100,000 fish tube, which enables migratory salmon, trout and eels to bypass the system safely.

Being so very long and narrow, the island's meandering central path hovers above the flowing river as it rushes by on both sides, and culminates in a cluster of tall, ancient poplars at its tip. The wind rustling through the poplars, combined with the sound of cascading water from the weirs, makes walking here a really pleasurable experience. The inner channel is also quite enchanting as it faces the beautiful lagoon formed by the weir and the neighbouring island.

Directly opposite the second Romney Eyot is **Cutler's Ait**. Another long and narrow uninhabited island, Cutler's Ait is joined to Romney Island by the large weir. It is very close to the Eton bank from which it is separated by a small channel and is crossed by two exquisite wooden humpbacked bridges. The ait is more densely wooded than its neighbours and is somewhat more interesting because it used to be a productive osier bed and the ancient Tangier Mill, recorded in the Domesday Book (1086), once stood on this island. Although the mill was demolished in 1899, the ait is still sometimes known as Tangier Island. The mill was once famous for its

Cutler's Ait, Eton.

production of high-quality clay smoking pipes. A large post at the upstream end of Cutler's Ait was known as the Abbot's Pile and was shown on maps as such. It was said to have marked the limit of certain fishing rights dating back to the time of tenth-century Merton Abbey.

The island is now owned by Eton College, which is situated across a field directly opposite, and although the exterior of the island looks much like any other willow-draped eyot, the interior has to be in the top five of the most beautiful of all Thames islands. The college's gardeners must be congratulated for having landscaped a series of delightful little gardens, each arrived at through a series of narrow pathways. Benches, begging quiet moments of reflection, are positioned at select vantage spots throughout the island, and here and there are little wooden pavilions, inscribed with meaningful Latin phrases, thus heightening the visitor's sense of the island's elite exclusivity. The downstream tip of the ait looking over to Romney Eyot and the lagoon created by the weir, is one of the most idyllic views on the Thames.

As the river flows under Windsor Bridge, a little island appears to be sailing towards you. This is **Firework Ait**. For all its size, this island is one of the cutest in the Thames. The tree-covered islet looks like a little boat crowded with willow passengers and commanded by a stately swamp cyprus tree with a delicate wild rambling rose decorating the prow. Firework Ait seems to have completely altered its position over the years, for maps of 1748 clearly show it closer to the Eton shore, whereas today it is much nearer the Windsor bank. A map of 1839 shows the ait to be about 150ft long by 35ft wide; on it stood a shed where a Mr Tolladay housed some boats. It used to be called Cooper's Ait, then Piper's Eyot and then Shampo's Island, after one Shampo Carter, a headmaster at Eton.

The island gained its current name from the grand fireworks display that used to be held on 4 June every year as part of the Eton Festival. By the late nineteenth century, however, this stretch of the river had become so crowded with pleasure boats, that on the 450th anniversary of the founding of Eton College in 1891, it was decided to transfer the annual Procession of Boats downstream to Romney Eyot. Consequently, Firework Ait was never used again and thus lost the reason for its name. For the next eighty years the little island became sorely neglected, becoming totally overgrown and an eyesore. Eventually, in 1971, it was restored and subsequently received a conservation award. Today it sits proudly as the centrepiece of Windsor's river scene.

A few yards along is another small island that never seems to have a name on any modern map, but on a map of 1798 it is called **Snap Ait**. Long and thin, Snap Ait virtually hugs the Windsor towpath from which it is separated by a tiny channel. It is lined with trees but the interior is thick with various shrubs that provide a welcoming home for wildfowl. There is also a small fishing jetty on the inner side.

The tip of Snap Ait almost touches the end of the next island, which has the gloomy title of **Deadwater Ait**. The centre of this large, uninhabited island is dominated by Brunel's handsome bridge, which carries the Great Western Railway on the branch line from Slough to Windsor. Under the bridge is a series of brick arches, one of the longest such brick viaducts anywhere in the world, and a unique example of industrial archaeology. The island is reached via a footbridge from the Windsor bank. It is almost enitrely parkland ringed with trees that form a small thicket at the downstream end.

Firework Ait, Windsor.

A map of 1798 shows the island as having three names: the lower portion is called Farm Ait; the centre, Dabchick Ait; and the top end, Jason Ait. It was also called 'Ackerman's Ait', presumably derived from a former owner or tenant. The backwater between this island and Snap Ait was known as the Deadwater, hence the island's modern name. At one time, however, around the 1860s it used to be called Baths Ait as it was a designated area that allowed local men and boys to swim in the river. In the 1930s it was enhanced by lining the banks with concrete, and hand rails were fitted along the waterline, together with changing rooms erected adjacent to the railway arches. Eventually, Windsor got a proper swimming pool on the mainland, and Deadwater Ait became a public park. At its downstream end the island narrows to a thin tail where there is a welcoming bench. Here, with the river lapping on both sides, the visitor can admire this wonderful setting with what must surely be the best view of Windsor Castle.

Just beyond Windsor and Eton Bypass Bridge lies the beautifully named **White Lillies Island**. This small, almost circular, tree-ringed island is reached by a road bridge from Clewer. It has the appearance of an exclusive enclave, and is sparsely inhabited by, presumably, very wealthy people. The island has around five or six very expensive houses that are separated by large gardens. They are set back from the river and all are gated, giving the island an unwelcoming feel. In 2001 the former *Neighbours* star and pop singer Natalie Imbruglia was living on the island and named her second album *White Lilies* after her island home. Although the small backwater is quite attractive, this island is distinctly lacking in atmosphere

The river now passes round the sharp bend of Windsor Racecourse, which, although technically an island, is only enclosed by the waters of the Thames on one side, with the Clewer Mill Stream on the other. Halfway along the racecourse's northern bank lies **Boveney Lock Island**.

Like many lock islands, Boveney was an island long before the current lock was opened in 1838. It is an ancient site that had a fishery recorded in 1205; a lock was first mentioned here in 1535. It is also shown as an island in plans of 1820 when it was known as Lady Caple's Ait. It is very small, shaped like a grain of rice with the lock and the keeper's cottage in the centre and pleasant gardens at each end.

At the mouth of the Clewer Mill Stream which leads to Windsor Racecourse marina, is **Bush Ait**. This tiny uninhabited island is densely wooded and is separated from the racecourse island by a very narrow but beautifully lush channel.

14

BRAY TO MAIDENHEAD

THIS NEXT LARGE group of thirteen islands begins on the reach around the Berkshire village of Bray, famous for its film studios, a religiously fickle vicar and lately for Michelin starred restaurants. On the left bank just before the first island stands Bray studios, where Hammer Horror movies such as *The Curse of Frankenstein* (1957) and *The Horror of Dracula* (1958) were made. The last Hammer production made at Bray was *The Mummy's Shroud*, which was completed in 1966. The studio building is a huge grey gloomy pile peering out from the otherwise charming riverbank. Although it is still used for music videos and TV productions, Bray Studios looks forlorn and quite spooky after dusk, as if the building itself was auditioning for a star role in one of the horror films. The first island in this group lying directly opposite Bray Marina is **Queen's Eyot**.

This long, narrow island of around 4 acres in size, sits almost in the centre of the river and can only be accessed by a private chain ferry. While both ends are quite densely wooded with some spectacular mature trees, the central section consists of a large, immaculately manicured lawn overlooked by a very attractive clubhouse that belongs to Eton College. The island received its name as long ago as the thirteenth century, when a grant of the manor of Bray was given to the Queen of England and wife of Edward I, Eleanor of Castile; from that time on, right up until the end of the nineteenth century, the island lay relatively ignored.

The eyot has been owned by Eton College since 1923 and has subsequently played an important part in the life of the school, which first acquired the leasehold of the island in 1898 from a Colonel Victor Van de Weyer who suggested that the college might find a use for it. Although the then headmaster of Eton, Dr Warre, went to visit the island on a wet and dreary afternoon when half the island was submerged, this did not put him off and the colonel's offer was accepted. He could not make a free gift of the island because there were restrictive covenants relating

to the property, but he granted a ninety-nine year lease for a peppercorn rent. Later, his son, Major William, overcame the legal restrictions when he succeeded to the estate so that through the exchange of ten shillings the island formerly became the property of Eton College in 1923.[1]

Shortly afterwards Dr Warre had a clubhouse built on the island to be used by the boys for recreational pursuits. Unfortunately, however, the attractive old clubhouse was totally destroyed in a fire in 1990, mercifully without loss of life. In its place a beautiful new clubhouse has been built from cedar and pine in a classical style, and is decorated throughout with memorabilia from the college's illustrious rowing history. Unlike its predecessor, the new clubhouse is not only for use by Eton pupils, but can also be hired out for special occasions such as parties and weddings. This is altogether a really beautiful isle with a wonderful mix of elegantly manicured gardens and an atmospheric wilderness at each end.

Continuing up river shortly after Summerleaze Bridge lies the famous **Monkey Island**. This sizable island of around 5 acres lies in a beautiful setting about a mile from Bray village. It is accessed by a footbridge across the immensely attractive back-channel and is home to a famous hotel with an intriguing history involving grotesquely painted monkeys and the Duke of Marlborough. It is generally assumed that the island takes its name from the unique monkey paintings in the island's Pavilion but this is incorrect, as the name is actually a corruption of Monk's Eyot. In 1361 the island was known as Bournhames Eyte, as before the Reformation the island formed part of the lands of the Abbey of Burnham, indicating that monks from the abbey were using the island in

The upstream tip of Monkey Island, Bray.

association with their fisheries on the Thames. Today, the river is higher than it was in those days, but the outline of the monks' fishing ponds, now reed covered, can still be seen.

The island may not have had much of a history had it not been for the Great Fire of London in 1666. To help in the rebuilding of the city, Berkshire stone was shipped downstream to the capital in barges, which upon their return carried rubble to be dumped on many of the islands on the Thames, thus providing Monkey Island with a solid foundation for building, as well as raising the island's height to eliminate serious flooding. The present inner channel was dredged and deepened in about 1775.

In 1723 Charles Spencer, the 3rd Duke of Marlborough, bought the island and erected two buildings described as a fishing lodge and fishing temple. The lodge (now the Pavilion) was built of wooden blocks cut to look like stone and still remains today in its original state. In 1738 the ceiling of the lodge was decorated with intriguing paintings depicting monkeys wearing gentlemen's clothes enjoying themselves in idyllic river scenes, either fishing, shooting, or boating. The artist was a Frenchman, Andien de Clermont, and the ceiling at Monkey Island represents his most inventive, striking and original work. An early visitor, Lady Hertford, didn't seem at all impressed with the duke's fishing retreat, however, writing to a friend: 'I went to see a little island which the duke has bought. He has a small house upon

Above *Monkey Island Hotel, Bray.*

Right *The interior of the pavilion on Monkey Island, Bray.*

101

it which has only one room besides a kitchen. The ceiling is painted with grotesque monkeys fishing and shooting. He cannot move upon the island without being seen by all the bargemen who pass, neither can he get out of reach of their bawdy conversation.'[2]

It seems the island was quite sparse and devoid of its present dense foliage, as Lady Hertford describes: '… except for six or eight walnut trees and a few orange trees in tubs, there is not a leaf upon the island: it arises entirely from the river running very much below its banks.' The Temple was originally open on the ground floor like a market stall and the attractive room above, once a billiard room, has a fine ceiling with Neptune, shells and mermaids in high relief plasterwork of Wedgwood style, which was completed in 1725.

Following the Duke's death in 1758, a succession of owners passed through the island. By 1840 the Pavilion had become a riverside inn, which became particularly popular after the turn of the century when fashionable society frequented the island. Edward II and Queen Alexandra often had afternoon tea on the lawns with their children, who included three future monarchs: George V, Edward VIII and George the VI. From 1912, H.G. Wells would often row up the river from the Royal Oak, his uncle's pub at Windsor, for trysts with Rebecca West, to whom the island was a magical place; she referred to it in her writing as 'the dark green grassy waters of an unvisited backwater.' West set much of her first novel *The Return of the Soldier* on Monkey Island, the heroine cast as 'the daughter of the man who keeps the inn at Monkey Island.' In July 1904, Sir Edward Elgar often visited the island while staying at Frank Shuster's country house, which sat directly opposite.

In 1956 a proper footbridge was built that physically connected the island to the south bank of the Thames for the first time. Until then the only means of getting to the island was by punt, which was run by an Irishman who had a dubious system for charging for his services. He would ferry visitors over to the island and then sit in the bar drinking at the rate of one Guinness per twenty minutes, provided by his customers. Should there not be a Guinness forthcoming at the prescribed time, he would ferry his boat back to the mainland and leave the visitors stranded.[3]

During the 1960s, the Temple was the private residence of Christopher Reynolds, who added additional rooms in 1963 while retaining the original building as a centrepiece. By 1986, however, the island and its buildings were in a very poor state. In that year the island was sold to Mr Basil Faidi, who restored the buildings as far as possible to their original condition. The result is the uniquely picturesque buildings that we see today, which have now been transformed into a discreet and unique hotel. The original fishing temples are now registered as Grade I listed buildings. In 1991 the Birmingham Six were spirited away in secrecy to spend their first night of freedom on Monkey Island.

Today, the area around the hotel is quite formal with sweeping lawns and a small putting green surrounded by some beautiful ornate trees and shrubs interspersed with oaks and willows and the ancient walnut trees mentioned by Lady Hertford back in 1738. The remaining two thirds of the island is fairly wild and unkempt, in fact, towards the downstream tip of the island it becomes almost impenetrable. With such a perfect habitat in such serene surroundings, tame rabbits scuttle about unconcerned by any human presence. In 2007 the island was sold to a Greek publisher for £7.5 million. The Temple building is still run as a very pleasant and successful hotel.

Passing under the M4 motorway, we come to a cluster of islands. The first of these is **Pigeonhill Eyot.** This long and narrow uninhabited island lies directly below Bray Lock amid beautiful bankside scenery. The eyot is heavily wooded and is separated from the southern river bank by just a very narrow channel. This area was a place of ancient settlement and Bronze Age artefacts have been found on and around the island. At its upstream tip is the dramatic weir adjoining the adjacent **Bray Lock Island**.

This heavily wooded little ait sits on the site of an ancient mill and is famous for its beautifully tended garden. In 1844 when a lock house was built on the eyot, it was known as Parton Ait, but an earlier name was Parting Eyot. The lock was built the following year.

Just a small channel separates Pigeonhill from **Headpile Eyot**. This larger island was once joined to Pigeonhill Eyot. Headpile Eyot is shaped like an ice-cream cone, wider at the downstream end and tapering to a fine point upstream where boats are moored. It is very thickly wooded and Bronze Age artefacts have also been discovered here. Both Pigeonhill and Headpile Eyots are rich in wildlife.

Rounding a bend, the river sweeps into Maidenhead.

A very early map of the Thames at Maidenhead in 1637 shows around twenty-two islands and islets from Climarch to Maidenhead Bridge. The islands were named as follows: (1) Climarsh Mead; (2) Norman's or Headpile; (3) Raye Eyote; (4) Turner's Mead; (5) Faire Waie Tarrs; (6) Cannon Eyote; (7) Peacock's Tarrs; (8) Woodmancotes Eyote; (9) Queen's or Ashen Eyote; (10) Horneyard;

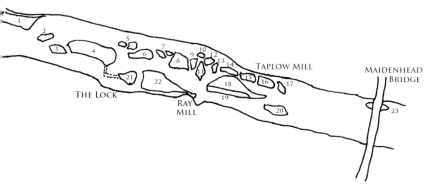

Map of the Thames at Maidenhead in 1637.

The old boathouse on Guard's Club Island, Maidenhead.

(11) Gladman's Eyote; (12) Little Tarr; (13) Great Tarr; (14) Teynter Eyote; (15) The Eight; (16) Flagge Eyote; (17) Cherry Tree; (18) Mill Mead; (19) New or Thorne Eyote; (20) Grasse Hill; (21) Raye Mill Eyote; and (22) Raye Mill Close.[4] It is difficult now to correctly identify all these islands but nevertheless, the map provides a graphic description of how the Thames islands have mutated over the centuries.

Today, within the boundaries of Maidenhead town there is a group of eight islands and islets that contains both the longest island on the river and one of the smallest. Just before entering Maidenhead we pass a tiny unnamed islet covered with a few huge trees, and then immediately ahead is **Guards Club Ait.**

This long, thin uninhabited island sits directly underneath Brunel's spectacular Railway Bridge. This was built in 1838 and allowed for the first railway connection between Maidenhead and London. It is an extremely innovative design with two of the largest and flattest arches ever constructed in brickwork, each with a span of 128ft. The huge arches sit astride the island giving it a slightly dark and haunting atmosphere. It was this bridge that inspired Turner to paint one of his most celebrated works, *Rain, Steam and Speed – The Great Western Railway*, which depicts a steam train rushing over the bridge.

Once known as Buck's Ait, the island gets its present name from the Guards Boat Club, which used to have its headquarters on this island. During the Edwardian era, this was the most exclusive boating club on the Thames. A unique ornate metal footbridge, built around 1865, led from the club's boathouse to the mainland. After the First World War, however, the island fell into disrepair and became totally overgrown. It remained a wilderness until the 1970s when it was restored (alongside some unkempt land lying directly opposite the island, which was turned into the small Guards Club Park) to commemorate the Silver Jubilee in 1977 and to provide recreation for officers who were stationed in Windsor and Pirbright.

There is little remaining of the boathouse today but its conical spire now covers the shelter in the park. The beautiful little bridge was eventually rescued and restored by Maidenhead Civic Society in 1976.

These days this lovely island has become a nature reserve that is strictly maintained for conservation purposes and is therefore closed to the public during the nesting season. Outside of these months, it is a real delight to step onto. Wild roses peep out of the foliage along a meandering path that runs the length of the island. Benches are placed at scenic vantage points and a little sandy beach invites a swim on a warm summer's day. Altogether, this is a very agreeable spot to rest up on a river journey.

Bridge Eyot, Maidenhead.

A little way past Maidenhead Bridge lies the unimaginatively named **Bridge Eyot**. This long, narrow, uninhabited island sits in the centre of the river and is completely covered in trees and ringed with some ropey-looking houseboats. It provides a dramatic introduction to a beautiful collection of islands running through Maidenhead.

Bridge Eyot is separated from the next island by tiny **Mill Ait,** which lies directly opposite Taplow Moorings. This attractive little ait was once much larger and is named after the large Taplow Paper Mill behind the moorings. It is reinforced with latticed wooden planks and is so tightly packed with small trees, shrubs and wild roses that it resembles a rather enthusiastic florist's wicker basket display.

A few yards along is **Grass Eyot**. This is another long, narrow, uninhabited island that is similar in size and shape to Bridge Eyot but in fact is much more impressive. Both Bridge Eyot and Grass Eyot are almost identical in size and shape and were probably one single island in the past. Both islands and Mill Ait, their cute little interloper, greatly enhance the aspect of the river as it flows through Maidenhead.

Grass Eyot is very inappropriately named, as it doesn't appear to have a single blade of grass upon it, although it most probably was once an osier bed. What it does have is a number of exceptionally large mature trees, including some of the tallest poplars to be seen on any Thames island. It has no moorings and there is no discernable way of gaining access, which is good given that it is an important undisturbed nesting site for wildfowl.

A short hop from the tip of Grass Eyot is a large area of land between the head of the Jubilee River and the Thames at Boulter's Lock called **Glen Island**.

This island stretches for almost a mile along the right-hand bank of the river just south of Grass Eyot to above Boulter's Lock Island, and is easily mistaken for the riverbank itself rather than an island. It is a strange shape: thick at each end and thin in the centre. The island was formed by the digging of the 'Mill Race', a channel to supply the paper mill at Taplow with water. The upstream end is covered in particularly lush woodland, while the central and southern tip of the island is given over to industrial buildings.

Looming up through the trees facing the main channel is the imposing gothic-like Glen Island House, built in 1869. This Grade II listed house, now offices for the paper mill, was built for Lt Gen. Sir Roger William Henry Palmer (1832–1910) an Irish landowner of considerable renown, who fought in several of the major battles of the Crimean War including the Charge of the Light Brigade. Later in life he spent a lot of time at Glen Island, where he kept several steam launches and devoted himself to Thames-side activities. The house was extended in 1884 and stands out as a good example of a mid-Victorian gentlemen's residence. It has been little altered since and the stained-glass window with the Palmer coat of arms can clearly be seen today.

The upper tip of Glen Island and the next two islands almost fill the river with one continuous land mass at this point, leaving just four narrow channels for the water to pass through. A huge weir joins Glen Island to the next eyot which is called **Ray Mill Island**.

This fair-sized island of 1.6 hectares is now a beautiful public garden with a menagerie of birds and small animals, and a small lagoon in its centre with some interesting statues dotted around. These include 'Vintage Boys' by Lydia Karpinska and 'The Companions' and 'Maiden with Swans' by Eunice Goodman. There is also a pleasant cafeteria. Everywhere there is the sound of water from the awesome Boulter's Weir at the northern end of the island.

The island takes its name from the Ray family who managed the flour mill here. The mill was constructed in 1726 on the site of a previous mill. In order to improve the adjacent Boulter's Lock, the Thames Conservators purchased Ray Mill Island in 1909, demolished the old mill and reconstructed the lock. Dismayed at all these new developments, Thacker mused nostalgically of how the pace of river life was changing in the wake of 'progress'. Of his discovery of an abandoned miller's cottage at Ray Mill Island, Thacker wrote:

> I roamed and dreamed over Ray Mill close one day in March 1912, while the new works were in progress; and discerned before it was too late what a little kingdom the island once formed for the sole and hand of a man. At the lower end was his material living, the mill: busy enough in old centuries when England was wise to feed herself; and close by stood his home. Here lay all his intercourse with the outside world. Within lay secluded an earthly paradise, surrounded with living Thames.[5]

Despite all this 'progress', it seems the island reverted back once more to nature, for in 1950 it was acquired by Maidenhead Borough Council who then cleared

Glen Island House, Glen Island, Maidenhead.

Ray Mill Island, Maidenhead.

the island of its dense undergrowth and turned it into the welcoming park we see today.

Lying adjacent to Ray Mill is **Boulter's Island**. This long thin island has the famous Boulter's Lock at its downstream tip, and is easily reached across a road bridge by the lock, which was constructed in 1772 and has a fall of almost 8ft, second only to Teddington Lock. This has always been one of the busiest locks on the Thames. There was once a Roman flour mill here but the first mention of the lock was in 1580–5 as 'Rea Locke' and later it was known as Ray Mill Lock. 'Boulter' is derived from the word 'bolter' meaning miller, and takes its name from the flour mill built on the island by the Ray family in 1726. Edward Gregory's famous 1895 painting *Boulter's Lock – Sunday afternoon*, which captured so brilliantly the late Victorian craze for boating on the Thames and the subsequent congestion on the lock, caused a sensation when it was exhibited at the Royal Academy in 1897.

The present lock was constructed in 1828 and the building, now known as Boulter's Inn, had been the mill owner's house until 1955 when it was converted into a bar and restaurant and the area between the bridge and the inn was sadly cleared of some splendid trees. The building was extended in 1961. There are a small number of attractive wooden houses clustered near the lock and some other secluded private residences further down the island. There is also a small boatyard. Before its conversion, the inn was the home of the BBC broadcaster Richard Dimbleby (1913–65). Apparently he often came out of his house and shouted at boats to slow down if they were travelling too fast along the river. As part of the Thames Salmon Rehabilitation Scheme, the last salmon ladder to be built on the Thames was opened at Boulter's Weir on 19 May 2000 by the Duke of Wellington. All the weirs from Teddington to Mapledurham now have salmon ladders, as these amazing fish are, alongside otters, returning to the Thames.

From Maidenhead the grandeur of the great loop of the Middle Thames to Marlow is scarcely surpassed anywhere on the river.

Launches waiting to enter Boulter's Lock with Glen Island in the background.

NOTES

1   For more information on Queen's Eyot see the Eton College website: www.etoncollege.com

2   Harwood, T.E., *Windsor Old and New* (published by the author, 1929) p.260

3   Thomas, G., 'Monkey Island', *Thames Valley Countryside*, Vol.8, No.30, autumn 1968, pp.58–9

4   Wilson, D., *The Making of the Middle Thames* (Spurbooks Ltd, 1977) p.60

5   Thacker, F. S., *The Thames Highway, vol.II, Locks and Weirs* (revised edition), (David & Charles, 1968) p.328

15

COOKHAM TO HAMBLEDEN LOCK

WE NOW COME to seven islands in the reach between Maidenhead and Cookham that is generally considered by many to be the most beautiful on the river. Here is arguably the loveliest scenery in the Thames Valley, as the river passes through the spectacular wooded Cliveden Reach, where steep chalk hills shrouded in luscious foliage and thick woodland rise up from the river's edge. The reach between Boulter's Lock and Cookham Lock is described by Jerome K. Jerome as 'unbroken loveliness this is, perhaps, the sweetest stretch of all the river', and the Cookham-born artist Stanley Spencer once said of the area: 'You can't walk by the river at Cliveden Reach and not believe in God.'

The first islands in Cliveden Reach itself are the evocatively named **Sloe Grove** or **Bavin's Gulls Islands.** This group of five small, uninhabited islands indeed appear as romantic as their modern names, although in the 1870s the islands were known by the less appealing name of Babham's Gulls. Three of the islands run down the centre of the river, while the other two lie close to the Cliveden bank. Although these islands are really only thin wooded strips, they are extremely attractive because they are so narrow: the sun and the light sparkles right through them leaving all three river channels bright and dappled, instead of the usual dark and gloomy inner channels.

Looking down on the islands from high on the wooded cliffs is Cliveden House. This graceful building was home to the Astor family, and in the 1960s was the centre of the notorious Profumo scandal. One of the islands, the first on the Cliveden side, is known as Picnic Island. This little gem has an inviting grassy centre flanked by clumps of small trees with the remains of campfires here and there. The sheer lushness of the surrounding scenery begs a stopover. The photographer Francis Frith captured the islet in 1890 when it was a favourite haunt of picnickers and the scene has hardly changed since. All five islands are part of the Cliveden

Estate and are owned by the National Trust. There can be no more perfect place for a picnic, and overnight mooring is permitted on all but the furthest isle upstream, which is a closed nature reserve.

As the river reaches Cookham Lock it splits into four separate channels. The right-hand branch was the original navigation channel known as Hedsor Water, while the two left-hand channels pass either side of **Formosa Island**.

This is one of the largest islands on the non-tidal Thames, covering 50 acres together with two smaller adjacent islands. Unlike neighbouring Sashes Island, Formosa was created naturally when the course of the river divided into separate streams. The channel to the south of the island was once the millstream used by Cookham Paper Mill, while the northern channel leads to Odney Weir. A survey map of 1808 clearly shows Cookham Lock Cut and it is clear how the present-day Formosa and Sashes islands were formed from a series of islands of varying sizes interspersed with numerous channels.[1] There are several buried channels running across the island that were connected to a medieval mill site, but they have long since silted up. The island used to be called Grannan's Eyot and belonged to a local fisherman when it was bought by the famous Admiral Sir George Young (1732–1810) for £50. He dumped tons of chalk on the island to provide a solid foundation for the large house he subsequently built and named 'Formosa', meaning 'beautiful Isle', because he once served off Formosa, now called Taiwan.

Formosa Island lies opposite Cliveden House. According to Henry Taunt: 'Formosa Island is not without beauty in its magnificent trees, but its situation in relation to the views obtained of Cliveden Woods, and the lake-like stream, which

The Sloe Grove Islands, with Picnic Island on the right, overlooked by Cliveden House.

runs at its feet is the finest on the river.'[2] Today the island can be reached by a footpath from Cookham. It is ringed by trees with a mainly open interior that is home to the Odney Club sports ground, as well as Formosa House, which is still owned by the Young family. A path crosses the whole island to the weir and then crosses the adjacent island to Sashes Island.

Crossing the weir on the north bank of Formosa Island we come to **Cookham Lock Island**. This very long, boomerang-shaped island is delightfully scenic. It used to be called Mill Eyot as it was once the site of the old Cookham Paper Mill. Although fairly wooded, there are lovely open patches of meadow and wild grassland interspersed with little tracks. A main pathway leads to Cookham Lock, which was excavated in 1829 along the course of an existing channel called the Sashes Stream, leaving the original course of the river to become a mere backwater.

Crossing the lock brings us to **Sashes Island**. This large island of around 23 acres is almost triangular in shape with another small, totally wooded islet to its north-west corner. The island is owned by the Environment Agency and the interior is open farmland ringed by trees, which is let on an agricultural tenancy. There is a campsite on the island that can be reached from Cookham over a footbridge, which crosses three channels of the river via Formosa Island and the lock island. Sashes was once known as Odney Island, but its present name derives from the Anglo-Saxon *Sceaftesege* or 'Sceaf's Isle'. A seventeenth-century map calls the island 'Shaftees' and there is also a record of a Shaftey's Ait just off Sashes Island.

The island was formed in 1829 when, in order to reduce the dangers of navigating the river at this point, Cookham Lock and a cut were created along the course of Sashes Stream. This is now known as Hedsor Water and has a functioning weir at its upper end and the remains of another weir at the lower end. Before the cut was made, an islet lay at the lower end of its site, which was purchased and dredged away by the Thames Commissioners. At the same time, Sashes Island was raised several feet from its original height by excavated sand and gravel, which was dumped on the island when the channel was dug to form the upper portion of the lock cut.

Cutting right across the island is a mysterious stream of which little is known apart from the fact that it shows up on the earliest known map of the island, which dates from 1580. The stream is hard to distinguish on the ground and only

really appears clearly in aerial photographs. Due to its strong natural defensive position, Sashes is an important site of ancient human settlement. Neolithic, Bronze Age, Roman and Anglo-Saxon remains have all been found on or around the island, and the dredging of the lock cut in 1856 uncovered a quantity of iron weapons dating from the Viking period. Further dredging in 1896 revealed a Danish winged axe and in 1958 a Danish spearhead was found during bank reinforcement work.

The north of Sashes Island is ringed by a ¾-mile bend in the natural mainstream of Hedsor Water, and on the opposite bank are the house and grounds known as Hedsor Wharf. It is hard to believe that this tranquil spot was once a hive of activity. For more than 500 years until the early nineteenth century, Hedsor Wharf was extremely important for local trade, with boats transporting coal, timber and paper to and from Cookham Paper Mill. This all came to an abrupt end when the lock was opened and Hedsor Water was blocked by the weir. All boats then had to bypass Hedsor Wharf as they headed for the new lock and, as a consequence, all trading ended on the wharf.

According to Thacker, between Cookham Bridge and Bourne End there were once four aits called Round, Great, Headpile and Cockmarsh Tarrs, none of which survive today. On the approach to Marlow, the river flows around the steep slopes of Winter Hill, which is thick with the trees of Quarry Wood. It was on this stretch of the Thames that Kenneth Grahame played during his childhood and in later life, in order to amuse his small son, he wrote *The Wind in the Willows* with Quarry Wood featuring as the 'Wild Wood'. Lying below Winter Hill, almost opposite Wooten's boatyard, are the **Gibraltar Islands**.

At first glance, these two islands appear as one because there is only a tiny channel separating them. In the past, there were more, smaller islands here upon which osiers were grown. Today, both islands are around an acre in size and are wooded around the perimeter with open grassland in the centre. There is a footbridge connecting the upstream island with the southern bank and on the same island there is a property called The Islands. It is rather an odd bungalow that looks like a store house, with municipal brickwork and a corrugated tin roof, but the gardens are a delight with a small swimming pool in an immaculate lawn; the rest is overgrown in a managed sort of way. The island is incredibly pretty with small fruit trees, rose bushes and shrubs alongside little meandering pathways. The Gibraltar Islands are a famous habitat of the Loddon Lily, an unusual species in this area.

Temple Lock Island near Hurley.

Hurley Lock Island, Hurley.

Lying directly under the Marlow Bypass Bridge is an unnamed island, which for the purposes of this book will be called **Bridge Eyot**.

A long, uninhabited island, Bridge Eyot is tapered in the middle and widens at each end. It is a pleasant place with boats moored on the inner channel and some splendid trees interspersed with patches of grassland, ideal for picnics. It is unusual for such a relatively large island to have no obvious name and I hope someone knows or will discover its real name and so give it a better one than I have.

A few yards along we come to **Marlow Lock Island**. This large and inhabited pasty-shaped island, attached to both Marlow Lock and Marlow's magnificent weir, forms the centrepiece of this pleasant town's riverscape. The island is traffic free and is reached by crossing over the lock from the Marlow bank. A pound lock was originally built here in 1773 and was replaced by a stone one in 1825; the present lock house was built in 1959. The upstream tip of the island is connected to the weir, while the majority of the sixteen or so houses are clustered near the downstream end. From the turn of the last century up until the 1980s, this was an extremely popular island for people to build weekend timber chalets, which have now been transformed into desirable and expensive permanent homes. In the 1990s the island was home to the writer Leslie Thomas, author of *The Virgin Soldiers*, who had intended just to spend weekends there but loved it so much that he and his wife moved to the island full time, spending weekends in London instead. The houses have large gardens fanning out into the island's centre, yet parts of the interior are left completely wild and impenetrable. Although not far away from Marlow town centre, this is a really secluded island that peacefully nestles away from the bustle around Marlow Bridge.

Rounding a sharp bend, the river flows past Bisham church where the water still washes over the bones of poor Mrs Edith Rosse, and one can reflect upon how far this graveyard really is from Thames Ditton. According to Thacker, towards the end of 1893 a small island at Bisham called The High Boughs was dredged away. Just before Temple Lock is **Temple Mill Island**.

This fair-sized inhabited island has unfortunately been developed into a rather bland, 1980s 'Brookside Close' housing development, which runs around most of the island's perimeter. The central section on the northern side has been excavated into a small marina. The island is connected to the Temple bank by a small road bridge; the road continues across the length of the island, the upstream end of which has thankfully been left tree covered.

The island is named after the Knights Templar, who owned the nearby Bisham estate. Later, monks from Bisham Abbey held the riverside Temple Mills as part of their estate. Although today it all looks rather suburban, the island's redevelopment is something of an improvement on the previous derelict mill site. The old mill was first used for corn milling, and in around 1710 it became a foundry for converting copper into brass. The mill closed in 1969 and the island and its buildings fell into disrepair until the mill was eventually demolished and the island was redeveloped into the houses and marina we see today. Temple Mill Island has a tiny private islet with just a handful of trees at its southern tip, which, at the time of writing, has recently been bought for £28,000 by someone who apparently wants to build a temple on it!

The southern tip of Temple Mill Island is connected to a dramatic weir that joins to the next island **Temple Lock Island.**

This very welcoming little island lies adjacent to the lock, built in 1773, and the Thames Path. It is partially wooded but has the usual immaculate lawn and flowerbeds that are associated with locks. The lock garden has won innumerable first prizes in garden competitions. Like many Thames lock islands, this little ait has witnessed tragedy. In the summer of 1888 the lock keeper's nine-year-old daughter fell from the small bridge on the lock gates and drowned. In 1908 Grace Simpkins, aged fourteen and the daughter of a later lock keeper, also drowned when a milk can she was carrying got caught up in her bicycle spokes and she was pitched into the lock waters. The son of another keeper also drowned here in 1917. On a happier note, with the stunning backdrop of Fultness Wood and a few benches strategically placed, these days it is a delightful place to watch the activity around the lock or to have homemade cakes in the lock keeper's cottage, which has been converted into a café with its own charming garden.

At Hurley the river widens to accommodate the next group of islands that are known collectively as the **Hurley Lock Islands**.

There are seven islands here of varying sizes clustered together and separated by very narrow channels. They are all uninhabited, traffic-free and very picturesque.

Here the water is crystal clear with inviting little sandy beaches, and the rare Loddon Lillies still grow in profusion. A mill at Hurley was mentioned in the Domesday Book but now only the mill race and the mill house remain. The islands are reached from the lock island nearest the Hurley bank or via two footbridges further upstream and downstream, which connect to the larger second island. The public have access to the first three islands, the rest are privately owned. The second island adjoining the little lock island is the least wooded of the group, being a mixture of light woodland and open meadows dotted with benches, picnic tables and brick barbeques. There is also a very decent café.

Because of their beauty and useful facilities, the islands are very popular with walkers, canoeists and other small boat users as well as campers. Indeed, a third island, called Camping Island, is designated for use solely by campers from April until September. This island is reached via a metal footbridge from the second island and has large family tents erected throughout the entire summer by the same families year after year. The first families came here from Paddington during the Second World War to escape the Blitz and some have been coming back ever since. One chap has been camping here since first being brought to the island as a boy, fifty-four years ago, and he says the island 'hasn't changed a bit' during those years.

The downstream Poisson Deux Island showing the spring display of white ramsons.

Nestling in the next bend of the river between Hurley Lock and Medmenham are the interestingly named **Poisson Deux Islands**.

These two relatively large uninhabited islands are thickly wooded around the perimeter with lighter foliage in the centre. In springtime they are carpeted in a sea of white ramsons – a cross between wild garlic and bluebells – and with various wildfowl sitting peacefully on their nests, it is a really pleasing sight. Outside of the nesting season, it is possible to land on the islands and picnic; some people even camp overnight.

There was once an ancient mill here called Frog's Mill, which was used by the French monks of the sixteenth-century Medmenham Abbey. Thacker mentions that these islands presented a problem to navigation because the towpath was on the other side of the islands from the main navigation channel. Hence tow lines had to sweep over the islands, often with the result that barges were pulled onto the shore.

There is a lot of confusion with the name of these islands because they are often referred to as Frog Mill Ait or the Black Boy Islands. Perhaps the term 'Frog' referred, in a derogative manner, to the abbey's French inhabitants, or perhaps it referenced the later aristocratic occupants who hosted the notorious Hell Fire Club

at Medmenham (the motto of which was '*Fay ce que voudras*' or 'Do what you like') with its sacrilegious and obscene orgies. One local legend, however, says that the islands are named after a boy bought back from Sierra Leone by a local gentleman, while another says the islands are named after Charles II, who was so dark as a child that his mother called him 'Black Boy'.

A plaque on some nearby cottage bears the inscription 'Poisson Duc', which is a corruption of a Norman-French phrase relating to a fish weir or duct. In 1950 Thames author L.T.C. Rolt was also confused by the island's name and wrote of how he believed they came to be so-called after hearing a local man refer to them as 'the Poison Ducks'.

At the time, the larger of the two islands was referred to on maps as Frog Mill Ait. So while travelling up river, Rolt was unable to pinpoint it on his map because he believed it to be a different island called the 'Poison Ducks'. As Rolt explained, the local man had said '"That's what we call it", yet could give no explanation of this most curious name. I had come to the conclusion that it must perpetuate some hoary Thames joke or some historic act of sabotage inspired by rural vendetta.'[3]

After some research, Mr Rolt discovered that the origin of the name was far more ancient, coming straight from (albeit slightly corrupted) the Norman-French of the Middle Ages. It records the fact that there was an ancient fish weir or duct

Magpie Island, Medmenham.

Meanwhile, the Thames meanders on through pastoral seclusion until it reaches **Magpie Island**.

Shaped like a willow leaf with a tiny islet at its upstream tip, this fairly large uninhabited island is very densely wooded. It used to belong to the Culham Court estate where it was used to trap eels. It is now a nature reserve and only accessible by boat.

At Hambledon Mill there are a group of islands known as the **Hambledon Lock Islands**. The river at Hambledon is broken up by three uninhabited islands between an amazing series of weirs. For once the islands aren't the scene stealers here, as the whole river scene is dominated by the striking weather-boarded mill, which dates from the sixteenth century, and the series of spectacular tumbling bay weirs. Hambledon Mill must be the best-known mill on the Thames, having been endlessly photographed, painted, sketched and used as a backdrop to countless advertising and publicity shots. The mill ceased working in 1955 and has since been converted into flats. The islands, although pleasant and wooded, are very much the backdrop here as they lack any dramatic tree line or interesting feature. What they do achieve, however, is help stagger the eye to take in the whole wonderful scene.

From Hambledon Lock the river sweeps in a great meander bend towards the genteel town of Henley-on-Thames.

at this place, probably set up by the Abbey of Medmenham. 'Centuries shrank at the thought that our friend had unwittingly used a term which the river folk first heard on the lips of a Cistercian monk from Normandy within a hundred years of the Conquest, and which they had crudely anglicised.'[4]

Whatever the name of these beautiful islands, I believe Frogmill, Black Boy and Poisson Deux all refer to the same two islands, and that the latter is the more attractive title.

NOTES

1   Wilson, D.G., *The Making of the Middle Thames* (Spurbooks Ltd, 1977) p.128
2   Read, S. (ed.), *The Thames of Henry Taunt* (Sutton Publishing, 1989) p.145
3   Rolt, L.T.C., *The Thames from Mouth to Source* (B.T. Batsford Ltd, 1951) p.37
4   *Ibid*, p.38

16

HENLEY TO SONNING

THERE ARE NINETEEN islands in this group, albeit many of them too small to merit much more than a name check. The first island, which sits squarely in the river's centre like a pointer to Henley town is **Temple Island**. This small island punches well above its weight in both local and national importance, as it marks the start of the Henley Regatta course, one of the most important social events in the English Season; thus it is sometimes known as Regatta Island. The island is mainly tree-covered but at its upstream end is the most exquisite little ornamental, eighteenth-century folly known as Fawley Temple, surrounded by an impeccably manicured garden with its ubiquitous weeping willow.

The island is named after nearby Fawley Court, designed by Sir Christopher Wren and built in 1684. It was later remodelled by the architect James Wyatt in 1771 for the court's then owner, Sambrooke Freeman, who wanted to incorporate the island into his ambitious garden design at Fawley Court; it was consequently known as Squire Freeman's Island. The temple was intended to be used as an ornate fishing lodge, with an interior based on designs which had recently been discovered at Pompeii, and was the first example in England of the form of ornamentation known as the Etruscan style. Over the years, like many a riverside folly, Temple Island fell into disrepair. In 1951 L.T.C. Rolt noted that: 'The little Classic "temple", which gives the island its name, looked sadly forlorn and dilapidated. It is to be hoped that someone will take it in hand before it is too late.'[1]

It took another thirty-six years, however, before the future of the island, including the Temple, was secured through the generosity of a Mr and Mrs Alan Burrough. Their magnificent donation in 1987 made it possible for Henley Royal Regatta to acquire a 999-year lease of the island from the then owner, Miss Mackenzie. Over the next three years a complex restoration programme was carried out, involving different experts at various stages. The Temple's interior imitates the antique plaques and large cameos produced by Wedgwood's factory at Etruria in Staffordshire. The wall paintings were thoughtfully and beautifully restored by Fiona Allardyce from 1988 to 1990.[2] Today, access to this unique and exclusive island, which can be hired for private and corporate events, is by boat, arranged with the regatta organisers. With its unsurpassed views of the mile-long run into Henley, this is one of the most beautiful islands on the Thames.

Passing under Henley Bridge we come to **East Eyot**. Arriving so soon after the elegant beauty of Temple Island, this small and narrow eyot appears distinctly dull in comparison to Temple Island. The island lies very close to the Henley bank and is sparsely wooded. It is uninhabited and at times, in winter, is almost entirely submerged in water. From a human point of view this is a particularly nondescript island, nevertheless it is popular with wildfowl and is sometimes called Bird Island.

A few yards along, almost opposite the famous River and Rowing Museum is **Rod Eyot**. There are a couple of minute tree-covered islets just before the tip of this very flat, oval-shaped island, which, like its neighbour, is prone to flooding so that its ten timber houses and chalets and a brick cottage are all built on stilts. Until 1907, when the town council sold off the plots, it was known as Corporation Island and then only the brick cottage existed, originally being the home of the farrier who

Temple Island, Henley-on-Thames.

shoed the barge horses. Today the island is sometimes called Town Rod Eyot, and whilst some of its properties are occupied on a permanent basis, most are weekend homes. This is a highly manicured island in beautiful surroundings in a privileged location, so although the island is only accessible by boat and occasionally completely floods, it remains a popular bolthole, even for locals. Indeed, one lady owns a house on Rod Eyot where she spends the summer, whilst in winter she moves to a flat half a mile away in Henley Town.

Within a few hundred yards are the **Marsh Lock Aits**. These two islands, set amid stunning scenery, have a complex lock and weir system linking them to each other and to both banks of the river. There are records of a lock and weir here from the early 1400s but the first pound lock was built in 1773. The lock with its neat little Georgian lockhouse was rebuilt again in 1914. Because the lock is unusually situated on the opposite side of the river to the towpath, two very long spectacular wooden walkways, with the huge weir situated between them, were built from the Oxfordshire bank to carry the path out to the lock island below the weir, and then back again to the riverbank above the weir. A salmon ladder was installed here in 1996.

The first of the two islands is the larger and used to be called Park Mill Eyot because it had four mills belonging to the nearby stately home Park Place, seat of the Earl of Malmsbury. On the Berkshire bank were two corn mills, and on the Oxfordshire side was a corn and paper mill. The second, smaller island is completely wooded. Back in the seventeenth and eighteenth centuries the lock was one of the busiest on the river with a wide range of goods such as wool, timber, grain and malt being carried to and from London in heavy barges. Today, this is one of the most spectacular settings on the Thames and a dramatic spot to have a picnic at the tables overlooking the weir.

On the reach above Marsh Lock between the villages of Shiplake and Wargrave, lie a chain of islands of which the first is **Ferry Eyot**.

This eyot is in fact three separate uninhabited islands: the largest is teardrop-shaped and there are two smaller islets at its upstream end. All three are thickly wooded. The island is named after the Bolney ferry that used to operate at this point carrying barge horses across to the towpath on the opposite side. At the time, the island was part of a collection of low-lying marshy islands one of which appears in a beautiful 1818 engraving by William Havell.

Next along is **Poplar Eyot**. A small oval-shaped island sitting bang in the middle of the river, it is uninhabited, inaccessible and heavily wooded. With no buildings on either side of the mainland banks, this is a very lonely and secluded island.

The next island in this chain is **Handbuck Eyot**. Another small and thin uninhabited island lying close to the Shiplake bank, this island used to be called Handbright Ait and again is a heavily wooded haven for wildlife.

Directly opposite Ferry, Poplar and Handbuck eyots lies **Wargrave Marsh Island**. This large area of former marshland is occupied at its upstream tip by the busy Willow Marina, but apart from a ribbon of very grand housing (that includes the home of the magician Paul Daniels) on the southern bank, it remains largely undeveloped. It is accessed by two small road bridges from the A321 over the beautiful mile and a quarter Hennerton Backwater. Wargrave Marsh became an island long ago when the meanderings of the River Loddon and the Thames formed this charming crystal clear backwater, which is spanned by a few little wooden humpbacked bridges. This is one of the loveliest backwaters on the Thames, and would naturally have silted up and disappeared long ago were it not for the Hennerton Backwater Association (HBA). This was founded in 2003 by local residents who cherished the tranquil beauty of this idyllic wildlife haven, and wanted to maintain and improve it. Until 1999, it was virtually unnavigable because it was almost entirely silted up. Since then, the HBA has worked to clear and maintain this delightful backwater so that the water now flows freely and small vessels can get through the very low Fiddlers Bridge at the upstream end.

For such a sophisticated and moneyed area, the island is unusually semi-wild and pastoral. A secluded farm squats amid a patchwork of flat unkempt fields and a central woodland shields a small, mysteriously deep black pond. It is very low-lying and there are masses of sheep. In fact, the whole island is reminiscent of Romney Marsh.

William Havell's 1818 painting of an Eyot near Park Place, Oxfordshire.

At the very tip of Wargrave Marsh is **Lashbrook Ait**. This small almost circular island takes up a good chunk of the river, leaving a tiny channel on the Wargrave side and not much more on the Shiplake side. This was once the site of the old Lashbrook ferry which stopped running because the towpath had to be relocated to the opposite bank to avoid just one house. The privately owned island is uninhabited and very thickly wooded. It is slightly mysterious looking with a dilapidated wooden chalet hidden among the trees.

Rounding a sharp bend and lying directly under Shiplake Railway Bridge is **Shiplake Bridge Ait.** This long, narrow uninhabited island sits close to the Wargrave bank to which it is connected by a footbridge. It is used for moorings at the upstream end, which is mostly open grassland, while the rest of this pretty island is sparsely tree-covered.

The next island, which adjoins Shiplake Lock, is **Shiplake Lock Ait**. A fairly large island, Shiplake Lock Ait is a very peculiar shape, in three sections. The first part is a thin strip of grassland with boats moored on both sides, which leads to a large oval-shaped centre with the lock on the Shiplake side; at the tip is a bridge to a further narrow section which in turn is linked to a small weir. Shiplake Lock has a long history: a mill and a weir were here before Norman times. By the end of the eighteenth century there were two mills here, one for corn and one for paper, but by 1907 both had fallen into decay and were demolished.[3]

Today the island is often known as Shiplake Lock Camping Island, as the central section of this ait is reserved entirely for campers, whose large family tents are scattered around the edge of the island. The rest of the ait is open grassland. There has been summer camping on Shiplake Island since 1889 when it was bought by the City of London, and despite periodic attempts by developers to purchase the island, camping continues today. As we have seen before with camping islands, each plot is handed down from generation to generation. Every April the wooden storage huts at the end of each tent are unpacked and the large tents are erected and filled with everything the family may need throughout the summer. The tents are surrounded by carefully tended flower beds, window boxes and tubs giving the whole island a wonderful splash of colour.

In a move harking back to the early island pioneers, often one or two family members, usually the grandparents, stay on the island the whole summer. This is no mean feat as the island has no mains gas or electricity; instead, candles and oil

Camping Island, Shiplake.

lamps are used for lighting and calor gas for cooking. One chap has been camping at Shiplake every summer since 1947. It is a fantastic place for children who, away from their TVs and computers, learn to swim from a very early age. They are also taught to fish and to row or punt on traditional river boats. As one resident said: 'We grew up without technology and we want our children to experience the freedom of this island and learn to have simple fun.' In mid-September, the tents and equipment are packed away on high shelves because the island often floods very badly. Opposite this island a branch of the River Loddon, famous for its lilies, or summer snowflakes, flows into the Thames.

A short distance upstream, opposite Shiplake College lies **Phillimore Island**. This delightful wooded islet sits in the middle of the river and is named after Sir Robert Phillimore, a politician, judge and friend of Prime Minister Gladstone; he lies buried in Shiplake churchyard. Another branch of the River Loddon also flows into the Thames opposite this island.

Phillimore's Island, Wargrave.

Around the next bend are two islands **The Lynch** and **Hallsmead Ait**. These two uninhabited islands are like twins and are always mentioned together. Both are large, almost identically triangular in shape and very thickly wooded. Where they differ slightly is that Hallsmead Ait is marginally bigger and provides moorings in the back channel.

Almost immediately a miniscule one-tree islet, possibly the smallest island in the Thames, is followed by **Buck Ait**. This tiny, uninhabited, willow-covered ait derives its name from the eel bucks or traps that were once placed here. It is separated from the mainland by a small channel.

Arriving at Sonning the river widens to accommodate the **Sonning Eyots**. Famed for its gentle surrounding slopes, the river at Sonning is broken up into a number of streams with islands in between. Here, between the two picturesque villages of Sonning and Sonning Eye, lie two large islands known as the Sonning Eyots and below them are two much smaller islands separated by an islet. A road bridge links the two villages and cuts across the larger islands. The first of these is private and ringed with trees, with just one large house amid a huge lawned centre.

The second island has a weir at its southern tip and is mostly wooded. On the northern corner there is an enormous eighteenth-century flour mill, which has been converted into a 200-seat theatre and restaurant. When the mill closed in 1969, it was one of the last flour mills on the Thames driven by water wheels. The new port mill at Tilbury had opened and Sonning, being much smaller, could not economically compete. Also, one of Sonning's major customers, Huntley and Palmers, stopped making biscuits in Reading. The mill remained empty and in a derelict state until 1977 when it was discovered by theatre lovers Tim and Eileen Richards, who converted it into a theatre and restaurant which opened in 1982. Today it is a flourishing and increasingly popular award-winning theatre in a wonderful island setting.

The two much smaller islands are thin and wooded. Both are uninhabited and one is joined to the Sonning Lock Island, half of which is occupied by a large private house with an immaculate garden. The other half the island contains the lock keeper's cottage and another well-maintained garden.

A short distance around a sharp bend, lies **Horden Ait**. This little cigar-shaped island sits in a lonely position opposite Caversham Lakes. It is uninhabited, thickly wooded and only accessible by boat.

The river now sweeps into Lower Caversham and the industrial sprawl of Reading.

NOTES

1   Rolt, L.T.C., *The Thames from Source to Sea* (B.T. Batsford Ltd, 1951) p.39

2   Orr, V., *Fawley Temple* (published by the stewards of Henley Royal Regatta, 1994) p.3

3   Livingston, H., *The Thames Path*: *Aerofilms Guide* (Ian Allan Publishing, 1993) p.113

17

READING TO PANGBOURNE

THERE ARE TEN islands in this group, five of them inhabited. The first is **Heron Island**.

This small island, shaped like a leg of mutton, lies very close to the Lower Caversham bank to which it is connected by a road bridge. It is almost entirely taken up with a rather dull development of 1980s riverside housing. This used to be the site of the ancient Caversham Mill, mentioned in the *Domesday Book*. According to historian Peter McGregor-Eadie, in 1493 Henry VII leased the manor of Caversham to the monks of Notley Abbey, and two watermills and a barge on the island were listed in the property. Around 1850 William Harvell, a well-known local artist, painted what by then was known as Caversham Mill Island, which is thought to have been as attractive as the famous mill at Mapledurham. People were still bringing sacks of corn to be ground here in the early nineteenth century and Caversham Mill did not finally close until 1929. The site of the mill was then redeveloped by the British Technical Cork Company, whose factory occupied the entire island. Before it was developed the island was a nesting ground for herons and so was given its current name in 1983 when the site was cleared and the housing development was built. The herons, unfortunately, lost their home and have since migrated to pastures new.

Directly opposite Heron Island lies **View Island**. This uninhabited island is slightly larger than Heron Island and is connected to it by a narrow bridge, but it is more commonly reached via a footbridge from the Thames Path at Caversham Lock. The path then crosses over a huge weir and onto the island. View Island gets its name from what used to be far-reaching scenic views of the Thames. During the daytime it is quiet and calm, part park, part nature reserve, with lots of open space, plenty of seating, a summer wildflower meadow, an education and picnic area and a canoe pontoon. It also contains several unusual wooden carved sculptures similar to those found on the South Sea Islands. Large unkempt grassy areas attract birds, mammals and aquatic creatures as well as damsel, dragonflies, and waterfowl. There are good examples of pollarded willows alongside small areas of woodland, as well as a wildlife pond which was created with a mix of shallow margins and deeper areas to maximise its wildlife value.

In 1914 part of View Island was removed so that Caversham Weir could be enlarged. In the 1960s, the island was a public park with a tennis court, but it was sorely neglected during the 1970s and '80s when the little bridge from Heron Island was falling apart and the island was used as a dumping ground. During this period, it was occupied by a large boatyard set amid scrub and wasteland but throughout the 1990s the boatyard became derelict and overgrown. Happily, in 1998 this forgotten island was granted a new lease of life when Reading Council began a clear-up operation to reclaim it as a public open space and to restore it to its former beauty. To protect the island from development, the council had gone to court in December 1997 to contest the previous tenant's application for a new lease. View Island had been closed to the public for more than thirty years since it was leased out as a private boatyard. Reading Council had to carry out a massive clearance operation, removing old concrete foundations from buildings, paths, crumbled tennis courts and rotting jetties, as well as general boatyard rubbish and chemical drums. It is therefore a significant and laudable achievement to have turned this island back into the recreational space and nature reserve we see today.

There are, however, several things that let this island down. Firstly, it has steep banks and dangerous river currents, plus a rule that no fishing or dogs are allowed on the island. Also, the downside of having such an accessible wilderness on the doorstep of a large urban area is that it can attract undesirables. In February 2011 the body of a thirty-three-year-old murdered man was found on a footpath on View Island. The death was drug-related and local people warn of the nuisance caused by drug dealing and general anti-social behaviour in the vicinity of the island. However, during the day, especially in warm weather, this is a place where families can bring young children and joggers trip over picnickers, much as they do in any other urban parkland.

The upstream end of View Island is connected to **De Bohun Island**. This long narrow island is also known as Caversham Lock Island because the lock and the large weir are connected to De Bohun Island. This must be the least picturesque lock on the Thames. There are no welcoming benches here, no little tea shop; in fact, the lock and the island are so unappealing that visitors are not encouraged to stay. Apparently, according to locals, anything pleasant left here would be destroyed by vandals.

Before the original lock was built in 1778, the island was called Blandy's Eyot after its then owner Edward Blandy. In 1816 the Thames Commissioners bought part of Blandy's Eyot from local landowner John Knollys for £200. At that time the eyot was in two parts: the main body of the island, and a small islet at the upstream end. A footpath linked the island to Caversham Mill via View Island. A photograph taken in 1965 still shows the island in two parts, but they are partially linked by a covered dock. Today the island contains a typical lock keeper's house, and until recently there was also a boatyard with a boat house used by the Environment Agency's river patrol and maintenance services. Sadly, the overall impression of the island is one of neglect. As of November 2007, proposals to redevelop the island and some adjoining land have been under discussion, but while negotiations stall, the island serves its purpose of getting boats through the lock, but otherwise continues its descent into unkempt shabbyness.

Passing under Reading Bridge, is **Fry's Island**. This large banana-shaped island forms the centrepiece of Reading's riverscape, and is only accessible by boat. It is sometimes known as De Montfort Island because it was the scene of a duel in 1163 between Robert de Montfort and Henry Earl of Essex. De Montfort had claimed that Henry was a traitor and demanded that the matter be settled with a duel on an island in the Thames. In the duel Essex fell and was thought to be mortally wounded, but he recovered at Reading Abbey and became a monk. A tithe map of 1839 shows the island as being owned by local landowner, John Knollys, who leased it to a John Fry from whom the island takes its name. It was then used for grazing cattle ferried across to the island.

According to historian Gillian Clarke, a map of Fry's Island dated 1892 shows that the downstream tip was then a separate islet of about 100ft by 90ft. It showed the centre plot owned by a George Lewis and the downstream one belonging to Reading Bowling Club, on the same site it has occupied since 1883. Around 1910 the gap between the islet and the main island was filled in. In 1892 Bill Moss became the lessee of the upstream part of Fry's Island, and used the island as a mooring for his fleet of small hire boats. He had plans for developing the island as a place for entertainment along the lines of Tagg's Island. He held riverside concerts and had the island profusely decorated with illuminated Chinese lanterns and myriad coloured lamps.[1] Eventually, as with Tagg's, the lure of the river as an entertainment destination waned and Moss concentrated on his boatyard business.

Today, the island is a busy place. The upstream end is occupied by the Island Bohemian Club, which has been on the island since it was formed in 1908 as a sports and social club where members could play bowls and tennis or swim from the island's designated bathing area facing the Caversham bank. It still continues as a bowling club. In the centre of the island is a large boatyard, but there has only ever been one private residence on the island, the attractive De Montefort House; it was built around 1897 on the downstream tip, and today is a beautiful white-painted residence.

A short way along, lying adjacent to Caversham Bridge, is **Pipers Island**. This small island is totally covered by a large, predominantly glass-built restaurant-cum-gastro pub called 'The Island'. It is reached via a staircase descending from the bridge onto a scruffy red-carpeted footbridge to the island. For many centuries a small medieval chapel stood on the island. This was replaced by the much photographed three-storey waterman's cottage, built in 1712. When the first Caversham Bridge was due to be replaced with an iron one in 1869, waterman James Piper and his family were living on the island and refused to move out. Using hydraulic jacks, the authorities finally moved the Piper family's cottage in its entirety to a safer site a few yards away. The house weighed 150 tons and the operation lasted three hours. Not a pane of glass was broken, and Pipers Island remains as a memorial to one of the most stubborn Victorian ferrymen in Caversham.[2] During the early part of the twentieth century, it was called Cawston's Island Lido and had numerous facilities for bathers, such as pontoons and diving platforms. In 1964 Cawston's wooden boathouse was replaced by a large attractive house and boatyard from which Piper's Island Pleasure boats operated.

In 2004 the island was bought for redevelopment. When demolition of the boathouse started on the island that summer, the previous owners were upset, believing that the work was unnecessary. Hazel McCluskey lived on the island in the 1960s with her parents and two sisters. They moved there in 1964 when their father Ronald Clibbon bought it and ran a successful boat-hire business from it for seventen years. He spent many years building the structure that was almost totally demolished by the developers. Mr Clibbon died in 1995 but his daughter said she was saddened and dismayed to hear of the new owner, Omer Yucel's, claims that the structure was unsound and could have collapsed in a storm. She told the local press that: '[My] father proudly built Piper's Island with a great deal of sweat and hard-earned money, and with regular visits from the planning office. It stood for over 30 years through floods, gales and storms – including the big one of 1987. How big a storm does he need to prove the structure was sound?' she asked.[3]

The matter was obviously controversial, given that the island's website says that 'due to foundation and structural problems the old building was demolished and rebuilt in its current contemporary style, taking advantage of the beautiful location and views of the river.' Despite the obvious expense involved in creating this striking glasshouse restaurant, it has a somewhat sterile atmosphere. With its great views, it is no doubt a fine venue for weddings and such functions, but for such a sophisticated-looking establishment it lacks character and, as a dining experience, it is a pity it could not devise a more inspiring menu.

In 1847 James Thorne in his *Rambles by Rivers* wrote of the next stretch of the river: 'The islands are a principal feature, and from their difference in size and character, some being large and clothed with rich foliage, others having but a tree or two, and some being bare or only covered with osiers and skirted with beds of rushes, are an extremely pleasing feature in the landscape.' The first of these islands so eloquently referred to by Thorne is called **St Mary's Island**.

A triangular-shaped uninhabited island, St Mary's Island sits close in to the northern bank in an area called The Fishery, with just a small channel separating it from the mainland. It is accessible only by boat and completely covered in woodland. This beautiful island is renowned for its wildlife. The Reading Amateur Regatta is held between St Mary's Island and Caversham each June.

On the river bend towards Tilehurst lie **Appletree Eyot** and **Poplar Eyot**. These two uninhabited islands are often paired together because they were once one long, thin eyot, but during the last century erosions have divided the island and Appletree Eyot is now only half the size of its upstream neighbour. The two islands sit right in the middle of the river so that navigation goes to each side of them according to the rules of the river. Both islands are densely wooded, and Poplar Eyot has a tiny islet at its upstream end and is a popular mooring place.

A little way along, across from Tilehurst on the opposite bank is **Roebuck Ait**. This diminutive little ait is separated from the northern bank of the river by a narrow channel. It is covered by relatively low-lying trees.

On the outskirts of Purley is **Ferry Eyot**. A tiny uninhabited island shaped like a grain of rice and heavily wooded, Ferry Eyot is named after the ferry which once crossed here to Mapledurham House lying opposite on the Oxfordshire bank.

Rounding a short bend is **Mapledurham Eyot** and **Mapledurham Lock Island**. These two islands are inextricably linked by the large weir that connects them, which is believed to date from the thirteenth century. Mapledurham Eyot is a remarkably attractive, almost completely circular island which is linked to the mainland via an equally beautiful old mill, which is the oldest working flour mill on the river. The island's upstream pointed tip connects to the weir, which in turn is connected to Mapledurham Lock Island. The lock was constructed in 1777 and became the first Thames lock to be mechanised in 1956. The lock island itself is pleasant enough, being just a small, thin, heavily reinforced strip of mainly grassland pockmarked with a few trees.

The staunch Roman Catholic Blount family bought the manor of Mapledurham in 1390 and at the time of the Spanish Armada in 1588, they built Mapledurham House, where their descendants still live. The house was used by John Galsworthy as a setting for *The Forsyte Saga*, and the 1976 film *The Eagle Has Landed*, starring Michael Caine, was filmed here, as were some episodes of *Inspector Morse*.

The picturesque channel between Whitchurch Mill Ait and Whitchurch Lock Ait.

Fry's Island, Reading.

A little way along is **Hardwick Ait**. This miniscule, almost circular islet sits bang in the middle of the river, opposite a wonderful little sandy beach on the Berkshire bank. The ait has just a couple of trees upon it. It is named after Hardwick House, thought to have been the inspiration for Toad Hall in *The Wind in the Willows*. It is one of the oldest houses in England, and stands a little to the north of the Oxfordshire bank.

Passing just under Whitchurch Bridge is **Whitchurch Mill Ait** and **Whitchurch Lock Ait**. This cluster of islands, two large and two small, sit in a wide bend in the river between the towns of Whitchurch-on-Thames in the north and Pangbourne in the south. The largest island, the Mill Ait, is joined to the Whitchurch bank by Whitchurch Mill. The mill is now a private house and the island is a beautiful garden, entirely tree covered apart from a lawn area adjacent to the mill. The island is joined to its southern neighbour by Whitchurch Lock, which in turn is joined to Whitchurch Lock Ait. Before the lock was built in 1787 these two larger aits were one single island that was cut in half to make the lock.

From the Lock Ait a large weir connects the island to Pangbourne.

The Lock Ait is also heavily wooded, apart from a garden clearing around the lock keeper's cottage. The weir forms a delightful lagoon with two tiny wooded eyots standing sentry-like at the entry of the lagoon. Beside the weir at Pangbourne is the luxurious boathouse where Jimmy Page and Robert Plant met to form Led Zeppelin in 1968. Page bought the boathouse for £6,000 in 1967 after it was converted into a residential dwelling. It is now for sale for £1.3 million!

It was here, at the Swan Inn opposite the Lock Ait, that Jerome K. Jerome and his companions finished their journey up the Thames.

The river now hurries along through deeply wooded hills towards the pretty Thameside villages of Goring and Streatley.

NOTES

1   Clarke,G., *Down by the River – The Thames and Kennet in Reading* (Two Rivers Press, 2009) pp.112–13

2   *Reading Evening Post*, 12 December 2007, p.31

3   *Ibid*., 5 August 2004, p.5

18

BASILDON TO ABINGDON

THERE ARE TWENTY-SIX islands in this long stretch, most of which are very small and uninhabited. Lying just above Beale Wildlife Park, against a backdrop of stunning scenery, are the two **Hartslock Aits**.

The first of these uninhabited islands is the larger of the two. Sitting in the centre of the river, it is long, narrow and densely wooded, with a path winding through the trees. The second islet is very small and thin and again tree-covered. Both these little islands are inaccessible except by boat. They lie in the shadows of the ancient Hartslock Wood, which cloaks the steep eastern slopes of the river, and from where the islands get their name.

The river then turns sharply left towards perhaps the most beautiful stretch of the Thames after Cliveden Woods. The twin villages of Goring and Streatley lie below the lovely chalk hills of the Chilterns, which frame a cluster of five islets just before Streatley. The first of these is **Gatehampton Eyot**.

This small and uninhabited triangular-shaped island snuggles into a bend in the river just past Brunel's Gatehampton Railway Bridge. It is completely wooded and hard to distinguish as an island because it is separated from the southern bank by the narrowest of channels. Small as it is, it has its own miniscule three-tree islet at its upstream tip.

A short distance upstream lie the **Grim's Ditch Eyots**. These three small wooded islets hug the southern river bank at a place called Grim's Ditch also known as

the Devil's Ditch. They are all roughly the same size, and until the late nineteenth century were one single island. The second of these islands has a slightly sinister feel, having an old Second World War pill box in its centre, now almost completely covered in foliage. Its dark hollow windows peer out unexpectedly from the dense thicket that covers the island, and the doorway beckons the unwary visitor into a dank black space. Altogether, this is not the most pleasant place to linger.

Grim's Ditch is a fascinating ancient earthwork in South Oxfordshire that is believed to date from the late Iron Age. It appears to be an unfinished attempt at building a defensive earthwork from Mongewell to Henley. The form this takes, however, is curious in that as well the main ditch there is a smaller enclosure where it meets the Thames itself. Here what is now thought to be a bridge was discovered leading to an island in the Thames where gold was being mined. It is thought that the Grimm's Ditch Aits once formed part of the larger island on which the gold was mined.[1]

The river now forms a large bulge as it enters Goring and Streatley. There are two islands here. The first is called **Heart Eyot**.

This fair-sized uninhabited island is in the perfect shape of a human heart, hence its name. It is an enticingly seductive island, being surrounded by a dense skirting of mature trees shielding a wild and secluded grassy interior. It can be accessed by a footbridge from the Streatley bank. At its north-western tip is a weir connecting it to the neighbouring island: **Swann Eyot.** This slightly smaller, triangular-shaped island is crossed by the Goring Bridge, built in 1923, which is actually two bridges that meet in the centre of the island. The eyot is named after the Swann family, who operated a ferry from here during the 1780s. The island is quite wooded with intermittent patches of grassland. The eyot has belonged to the Swan Hotel on the Streatley bank for as long as anyone can remember. There are moorings along the western side of the eyot, and because the island floods occasionally, only the boat's occupants are allowed access to the island. Hotel staff visit the island twice a year to mow the grass, but other than that it is left alone as a wildlife haven.

Moments up from Goring Lock are the **Cleve Eyots**. There are three islands here that before the mid-nineteenth century were one large eyot. Only one is inhabited. The first and largest ait is around 2 acres in size and is shaped like a headless kipper. It is uninhabited and heavily wooded. The second, much smaller, ait is also tree-covered, and its horseshoe shape has created a lagoon at its southern end where there is also a house. A small weir at the northern tip connects to the third island. This triangular-shaped ait of around 1.5 acres is called Cleve Island. It is a private island and until recently was owned by the rock musician Pete Townshend of The Who. The island has a little sandy beach at its southern end as well as a mooring platform, and informal pedestrian access over Cleve Lock. At the northern tip a larger weir connects to the lock island. These islands have a beautiful outlook across the Berkshire Downs.

Half a mile or so along is one of the tiniest islets on the Thames, which is merely a little mudflat with a couple of small trees. Then, shortly before the famous Beetle and Wedge Inn, on the Moulsford bank, there is a splendid art deco house designed by the architect John Outram in an Egyptian style. Lying just above Brunel's spectacular 1839 masterpiece, Moulsford Railway Bridge, are the **Moulsford Eyots**.

The three uninhabited islands in this group are only accessible by boat. The first island is the smallest and, as usual, is completely tree-covered. Its tip almost touches the next two larger islands, which lie adjacent to each other with just a very narrow, gloomy sunless channel between them. Again they are densely wooded with ancient crack willows. This is a very lonely stretch of the river, so it is not surprising to hear that the Moulsford islands are thought to be haunted. The four thick arches of the bridge cast a long shadow over these isolated islands and as you explore there seems to be a mist hanging over them no matter how sunny a day it is.

A straight run up through Wallingford brings us to **Benson's Eyot**. This really beautiful, pear-shaped island lies close to the Benson bank. For once, here is a fair-sized island that is not entirely covered in trees. There are some, but they are scattered thinly along the perimeter, while the centre is grassland. Midway along the eastern bank is a footbridge over to another tiny grassy ait, which has a handful of trees. This little island within an island is like finding something precious in your pocket, as it is so tucked away and hidden. At the northern tip of Benson's Eyot is a huge weir connecting the island with **Benson's Lock Island.** This lock ait looks like an airstrip with a wide centre and two long thin grassy strips jutting out at both ends. The lock, first built in 1788, occupies the site of an ancient weir and watermill.

Another long stretch without any islands until a dramatic angular bend in the river opposite the village of Little Wittenham is filled with **Lock House Island**.

This sizeable, inhabited, boomerang-shaped eyot sits in the centre of the river, and is crossed by an attractive ornate footbridge that spans the river in two sections with Lock House Island in between. The lock house was built in 1928 and is situated in the centre of this lovely island. From April until October there are camping pitches on the island, and the little arched bridge, so near in appearance to E.H. Shepard's famous drawings, is used in the heats and the final of the World Poohsticks Championships.

A few yards along is **Day's Lock Island**. This strangely long, very thin island is laid mainly to grass and pockmarked with the odd tree. Day's Lock was first built in 1789 and was rebuilt in 1871. The lock is situated on the eastern side and on the opposite side the weir joins the island to the Wittenham bank.

The river now loops around a large chunk of flat agricultural land to two islands called **Clifton Lock Island** and **Clifton Cut Island**.

The small lock ait is merely the bisected tip of the Clifton Cut. This is a man-made island that was created at the same time as the lock in 1822 by a long cut being dug to speed up passage towards Clifton Hampden while the winding old course of the river passes the edge of Long Whittenham. The lock was built in 1822 on the site of the old Clifton ferry. The island houses the lock keeper's cottage and its neatly tended gardens. At its southern end a small weir joins to the large elongated chunk of Clifton Cut Island opposite the village of Long Wittenham. This uninhabited island looks like a leg of mutton and is comprised entirely of grazing land, with some enticing little sandy beaches and a weir connecting to the Wittenham bank.

The river then runs without bend or curve towards another, similar sized, man-made island called **Culham Island**. This very large, oblong-shaped uninhabited island was formed when a cut was created in 1809 in order to bypass a difficult meandering bend in the river, and also to bypass Sutton Mill with its weirs and weir pools, which slowed the passage of barge traffic. The weir pools are now known as Sutton Pools and lie off the southern bank of the island. They are stunningly scenic with a series of small tumbling bays cascading into three tree-ringed inky-green pools. The lush foliage along the banks of the pools occasionally gives way to little shingle beaches and rocky outlets, which are ideal spots for anglers. The downstream tip of the island is crossed by Culham Bridge. The main navigable route of the Thames is through the Culham Cut, though the old course meanders to the south past the village of Sutton Courteney, one of the loveliest on the Thames and the burial place of George Orwell (1903–50). It is possible to walk from Sutton Courteney village across all the weirs onto Culham Island itself, which is almost entirely agricultural land. A footpath cuts right across the island to a small footbridge leading to Culham village.

Passing through Cullham Reach, a narrow channel appears on the right that marks the beginning of **Andersey Island.** One of the largest islands on the Thames, its 273 acres are separated from the mainland by a narrow channel called the Swift Ditch, or sometimes referred to as Black Water. The island is primarily a vast expanse of agricultural land with some wild meadows and woodland around the perimeter. Despite the busy A415 crossing the eastern half of the island, this is a really pleasant, pastoral place to walk along the towpath facing Abingdon town. On its western edge the island contains a football club, a cricket club, a leisure facility and towards the centre there is an old farm and some cottages, possibly the 'Rye or Rivy Farm, a house of great antiquarian interest' mentioned by Thacker. The island of Andersey was the site of a royal residence as early as Anglo-Saxon times, and was taken over by William I. The site was later acquired by the Abbot of Abingdon in about 1100 but over time the buildings gradually fell to ruin.

The course of the Thames around the town of Abingdon has undergone some interesting changes over time. Historically, the Swift Ditch was referred to as the 'Chefe Streme' and was the only navigable channel of the river in the vicinity of Abingdon; as a result it isolated the town. Andersey Island was created during the years AD 955 to 963, when the course of the river was divided into separate streams by the monks of Abingdon Abbey, founded in AD 675, to aid their industry and cleanliness. This piece of ancient monastic engineering now forms the most northerly channel of the river at Abingdon and is called the Abbey Stream, while the main course of the Thames runs through Abingdon and the old historic route of the river is relegated to the narrow cut known as Swift Ditch.[2]

To improve the river trade in Abingdon in around 1052, the monks dug out a new channel to further divert the river. Nevertheless, Swift Ditch was to remain the main navigable channel until around 1790, when Abingdon Pound Lock was built and the channel through Abingdon town was widened to accommodate more river traffic. Looking at the Swift Ditch today, it is hard to imagine that this insignificant, overgrown backwater once formed the sole course of the Thames.

Lying directly in the middle of the two Abingdon bridges is **Nag's Head Island**. This fair-sized island has its upstream end totally bisected by the road bridge carrying the busy A415 through Abingdon, the oldest continually inhabited town in Britain. The island fills a wide bulge in the river but is fairly unremarkable, with pleasant open grassland dotted with rose bushes, some huge conical conifers and two large willows cloaking the downstream tip. Boats are moored around the perimeter and several boat-related businesses occupy the island's southern bank. From here a daily river boat service runs to Oxford. At the northern end is the old Nag's Head pub which gives the island its name. Sadly this has been abandoned and boarded up for almost a year. This part of the island is cut in half by a small channel, with the pub's foundations actually in the river. The most wonderful thing about this island is the view of the beautiful original Abingdon Bridge, built in 1416 with its graceful arches running across the inner channel.

Immediately to the left of Nag's head Island is **Abbey Island**. This large triangular-shaped island is separated from the Abingdon bank by the Abbey

Abingdon Bridge crossing over Nag's Head Island, Abingdon.

Stream. It can be accessed from numerous little footbridges and from the weir crossing at its north-eastern tip. The southern end is occupied by a large hotel but the major part of the island is open meadowland scattered with trees, including two long rows of giant Lombardy poplars, their old grey trunks looking like the cloisters of some ancient monastery. The island serves as a popular public park with an open-air swimming pool, tennis courts and the few remains of Abingdon Abbey in the centre, which today contain a reconstruction of an Elizabethan theatre. The tree-lined inner channel is delightful and a small wooded islet lies off the southern bank.

The northern tip of Abbey Island is connected to a weir and footbridge leading to **Abingdon Lock Island**. A charming picturesque island, Abingdon Lock Island is like a miniature version of Abbey Island with a mixture of grass and woodland interspersed with little pathways. The lock, built in 1790, lies adjacent to the bank of Andersey Island. Although a path cuts through the island to the large weir crossing to Abbey Island, this little island is a worthy destination in itself, and is arguably the most scenic spot in the Abingdon stretch of the river.

Leaving Abingdon we now enter a particularly lovely reach with Lock Wood on the right and at its end **Lock Wood Island**.

This small heart-shaped island almost fills the river, with the main channel only a little wider than the backwater. It is very attractive, being thickly covered with mature trees and linked to the wooded slopes of nearby Nuneham Park. The island and the adjacent wood were named after a flash weir that once stood on this part of the river. In the nineteenth century there was a thatched cottage on the island that was accessed by a rustic bridge and was popular for picnickers. Apparently, Alice Liddell used to visit the island with Lewis Carroll, who penned *Through the Looking Glass* shortly after one of these visits.

In the run up to Oxford, the river passes through unremarkable pastoral scenery until it reaches the famous lock at Sandford-on-Thames.

NOTES

1   '12,000 years of the Goring Gap', www.historicenvironment.co.uk

2   For a detailed discussion on the division of the River Thames at Andersey Island see: Thacker, F.S., *The Thames Highway: vol.II Locks and Weirs* (David & Charles, 1968) pp.143–52

19

SANDFORD TO ST JOHN'S ISLAND

THE TWENTY-FOUR ISLANDS in this last group are, in the main, lock islands that were natural islands before the locks were built. Those past the town of Oxford are largely characterised by their lonely isolation, amid the huge empty water meadows that accompany the river to its source. The first islands in this group are **Sandford Eyot** and **Fiddler's Elbow**.

These two large, uninhabited islands, separated by a narrow channel, form a wonderfully curving landform that slithers along the riverbank for almost a quarter of a mile. Sandford Eyot's graceful curve ends in a sharp point at the downstream end, across which is a footbridge connecting it to Sandford Lock with its impressive mill buildings. These were originally built by the Knights Templar in the thirteenth century, and are now converted into desirable flats. The island is predominantly open meadowland and two small weir streams bisect the upper end, thus creating two additional smaller islands. Sandford Lock, which existed as early as the 1620s, is the deepest lock on the Thames above Teddington with a fall of 8ft 10in, and it can be a very dangerous place.

The area of water trapped between the eyot, the Kennington bank and the notoriously ferocious weir known as the Sandford Lasher, is known as Sandford Pool, and was described by Jerome K. Jerome as 'a very good place to drown yourself in'. The pool, which looks so inviting for a swim on a warm summer's day, has unpredictably treacherous undercurrents and over the years a good number of people have indeed drowned here. A memorial stone obelisk with the names of some of those who perished stands on the 'Lasher' where most of the lives have been lost. Among these were two Oxford students from Christchurch College, Richard Phillimore and William Gaisford, who drowned in 1843. Three other Christchurch men also lost their lives here. George Dasent drowned in 1872, while Michael Llewelyn Davies and Rupert Buxton drowned in 1921. Llewelyn

Davies was the adopted son of J.M. Barrie, and is believed to have been the inspiration for the character of Michael in *Peter Pan*. Since then many more have perished, yet it seems odd that so many who drowned should have come from Christchurch College.

Fidler's Elbow is altogether a safer place, having just a narrow calm backwater. The island is shaped like of a leg of lamb, with a wide expanse tapering upstream where a footbridge links it to the Kennington bank. The island's centre is mainly meadowland ringed with trees and shrubs. Altogether, provided you don't swim in the Pool, these two islands are both very scenic and interesting to explore.

There follows a very sharp bend almost half way between Sandford and Iffley Locks in which lies **Rose Island**. This beautiful little privately owned island, almost square in shape, is heavily wooded and is linked to the mainland by a rustic wooden footbridge over a delightful back channel. It was once known as both Kennington Island and Saint Michael's Island, although there is no church of that name in the nearby vicinity. The island's solitary house stands on the site of a once-popular pink-washed inn called The Swan. In the 1920s it became an hotel and has been a private house dominated by a splendid Lebanese Cedar, since just before the Second World War. According to the owner, parts of the building are half-timbered with wattle and daub infill, and the wooden beams have been dated to the 1500s. The rest is early Victorian extensions.

According to research done by the owner's family, the first mention of the island in the Oxfordshire Records Office was the name of the innkeeper in 1596. Also, there are unconfirmed accounts that it was named as part of the local estates of the Knights Templar. It seems possible that there was a hostelry or at least a dwelling of some sort as early as the thirteenth century. As a pub it is featured in *Tom Brown at Oxford*, the sequel to *Tom Brown's Schooldays*. Tom rows down to the pub on his first trip on the river. It was also the destination of the first trip on which Lewis Carroll was allowed to take Alice Liddell and her siblings out without escort.

Passing under Kennington Railway Bridge, just beyond Isis Bridge is **Iffley Lock Island**. This small ship-shaped island sits squarely in the centre of the river, with its western bank joined to the ancient Iffley Lock. On the other side a bridge straddles the old mill stream to Iffley village. Along with Sandford, this is one of the pioneering locks on the Thames as there has been a lock on this site since at least 1632. The present lock dates from 1924. The island is named after the extremely picturesque Iffley Mill that once stood close by and was apparently, along with Hambledon Mill, the most painted and photographed mill on the Thames. Indeed, Charles Dickens Jr, writing in 1888, noted that: 'It is hardly necessary to visit Iffley to see the Mill. It has been painted in every kind of medium. Rarely is there an exhibition at the Royal Academy … or any of the watercolour societies, without at least one piece from Iffley.' Sadly, the thirteenth-century mill was destroyed by fire in 1908, but a part of it was rebuilt as a nearby house called Grist Cottage.

A short distance upstream brings us to Oxford's gateway and to **Grandpont Island**. This unusual island is situated south of Christchurch College and is crossed by a beautiful stone bridge called Folly Bridge, or Grand Pont. It is believed that the first known stone bridge was built around 1085 on the site of an earlier timber Saxon bridge. The Norman bridge survived until the present bridge was erected in two parts between 1825 and 1827, and was separated by Grandpont Island. There was once a mill on the island that has long since disappeared. Sir Francis Bacon lived in the old drawbridge gatehouse which gives the bridge its name, although the building was demolished in 1779.

The island itself is quite small and is entirely built over with five large buildings: three on its larger upstream section and two on the downstream part. Collectively they are an odd hotchpotch of architectural styles and periods. As author Christopher Winn noted, the most interesting building on the island is No.5 Folly Bridge, a red-brick castellated house festooned with cast-iron balconies and

niches filled with statues, allegedly representing the fallen women who worked there when the place was a brothel. In 1911 it became rather more respectable as the home of science historian Robert Gunther, founder of Oxford's Museum of the History of Science.[1] The foundations of this ornamental folly are buried deep in the river and the side of the house is lined with punts and skiffs. Behind the house a restaurant gives out onto a canopied wooden platform with tables and seating overlooking the river and a gondola moored alongside. Thus, a faint air of Venice pervades this part of the island. Meanwhile the two properties on the downstream section are distinctly Victorian in appearance. From here a pontoon bridge leads out to several pleasure boats which can be hired.

A little further along are a group of three islands called the **Osney Aits**. The first of these is an extremely long, thin, gracefully curved island, which is almost entirely grassland ringed with trees on the outer bank and moorings on the inner. At its northern end is the site of the old disused Osney flour mill. A footbridge connects the island to the smaller lock island, which is developed with various light industrial buildings. The lock was built in 1790 and to the north of the island is a weir with a footbridge leading to a very small islet with another smaller weir. This forms the top of the Osney Weir Pool, with its dramatic crescendo of water cascading into a dangerous-looking whirlpool.

Onwards under Osney Bridge, alongside the ancient common land called Port Meadow, is **Fiddler's Island** and **Medley Eyot**.

Fiddler's Island can just about be called an island, as its southern side is just separated from the mainland by a short narrow stream called the Sheepwash Channel. It is a fair-sized, long, very attractive island with a mixture of wood and grassland. It used to be grazing land but has now gone 'native' with tall willowherb and reeds making it a wonderful wildlife refuge. A path runs its entire length and connects to another smaller, very thin island called Medley Eyot. The name 'Medley' comes from 'middle island' as Medley Island lies between Osney and Bisney. The island is merely a grassy strip with some trees and moorings along its eastern bank. It is reached via two footbridges, one at each end of the island, the upstream one being the more attractive gracefully arched and latticed 'Rainbow Bridge', built in 1865.

Grand Pont Island, Oxford.

SANDFORD TO ST JOHN'S ISLAND

Next along are the **Godstow Eyots**. These two aits lie in a beautiful and interesting patch of the Thames opposite the huge flat expanse of Port Meadow. The first of these two aits is the smaller Godstow Lock Island with its welcoming, wonderfully colourful lock garden. The lock was constructed in 1790 and the island is a mix of grass and small trees and has just one property. On the lock-side mainland bank lie the ruins of Godstow nunnery, founded in 1133, which was largely destroyed by parliamentary forces during the Civil War in 1645. All that remains of the nunnery is its large walled enclosure and the ruins of a small sixteenth-century chapel. At the top of the Godstow Lock Island is a tiny weir connecting it to the much larger, half-moon-shaped Godstow Eyot.

This fairly well-wooded island is interspersed with patches of open grassland. The beautiful stone Godstow Bridge, built in 1792, crosses the northern tip of the island over a weir. The famous Trout Inn, which stands at the end of the bridge overlooking the weir, was first built in 1138 as the hospice for the Godstow nunnery. When workmen were digging out the cut for the lock they uncovered the grave of the prioress of the nunnery. The Trout Inn, in its stunning setting, was often frequented by Colin Dexter's much-loved fictional detective, Inspector Morse.

On a sharp bend in the river at Wolvercote lies **King's Eyot**. A fair-sized triangular-shaped island, it fills a large bulge in the river and is mainly wooded with pockets of grassland and a narrow channel slicing across its western side. At its eastern corner is King's Weir linking it to Pixey Mead on the mainland, while King's Lock is situated on the island's southern bank. The old flash weir at King's Lock is mentioned in 1541 and by 1791 belonged to the Duke of Marlborough, who apparently never collected any tolls and neglected the site, which by 1882 lay in ruins. The weir was rebuilt and enlarged in 1885 and there were constant demands for a lock so one was eventually constructed in 1928. This really is a beautiful, secluded island, uninhabited apart from the lock keeper's cottage with its immaculately kept gardens and picnic benches.

The river now reaches its northernmost point as it turns on past the 600-acre Wytham Great Wood to **Eynsham Eyot**. This is another smaller triangular-shaped island with a weir and a lock on its southern bank. The present lock was completed in 1928, and along with King's, is one of the very last to be built on the Thames. A small footbridge connects it to the Swinford bank. This picturesque little island is mainly open grassland with a few small trees scattered about and is a popular place for mooring and picnicking.

Passing under Swinford Toll Bridge, built in 1777 and one of the most beautiful on the river, lies **Swinford Eyot**.

This small, almost circular island is chiselled out of the Eynsham riverbank by the narrowest of channels. It is privately owned and contains one of the most secluded properties on the Thames. In the centre of the island sits one solitary house complete with helipad, which is reached down a road leading solely to this island across a small bridge.

Here the river twists and turns until it reaches **Pinkhill Eyot**. This small, pear-shaped island almost completely fills a bulge in the river. It is lightly wooded with a tiny weir at its southern tip and a lock on its eastern bank. The original lock was built in 1791 and rebuilt in 1877 and again in 1898. In 1909 a Mr H. Smith was appointed lock keeper. He cleared the lock island of its vegetation and in 1910 won the prize for the best-kept lock on the river. No doubt the garden was a model for the neat, manicured little garden displays we see and admire at most locks these days. Thacker, however, disapproved of the mass clearance of these lock islands, preferring the 'olde world' cottage gardens that grew up around the original keeper's cottages. Of the old garden at Pinkhill he wrote affectionately of '…the rambling wilderness of a garden, full of vegetable patches and familiar old world flowers, crowded in summer with scores of campers.' Today the visitor is greeted by an idyllic island with a beautiful colourful lock garden, worthy of Mr Smith, complete with picnic area.

There is now a long islandless stretch before reaching **Northmore Eyot**. This remote island is shaped like a small boat and has a large weir at its southern tip. The lock was built in 1896 to replace the old Hart's weir, named after a William Hart, whose family had owned a fishery here from the 1740s. It is one of only three paddle and rymer manually operated weirs left on the Thames: the others are Rushey and

Radcot.[2] Despite having a couple of picnic tables, it is, nevertheless a fairly dull little island with just four trees amid a patch of grass.

The river continues along another really long stretch through empty countryside, before the appearance of **Shifford Island**.

This large island was formed by the Shifford Cut, dug in 1896–7 to ease navigation and avoid the loop of the river to the south, which is itself distorted by tortuous meanders within the meander. In doing so, the cut created Shifford Island; the lock was built the following year in 1898. The island is uninhabited and is comprised of a patchwork of small fields surrounded by a peaceful backwater, part of which remains navigable by small craft to Duxford ford, the last surviving purpose-built ford on the river, and the only one not to have been replaced by a bridge or a lock. Shifford is often described as the loneliest lock on the Thames. Indeed, apart from a couple of tiny hamlets, this is possibly the most remote and isolated reach on the entire river.

Around several more tortuous bends and under the quaint eighteenth-century Tadpole Bridge, lies **Rushey Lock Island**.

Here is another island set in splendid isolation. Shaped like a small elongated triangle, it has a lock which opened in 1790 on its northern bank, and a dramatic weir on its southern bank. Rushey is the oldest surviving paddle and rymer weir in the country. This is a very picturesque little island with its lock keeper's house crowned with a pyramidical roof built in 1894, and well-kept gardens complete with picnic tables.

The river now zigzags its way along to **Radcot Lock Island**. This little lock island is shaped like a sugar mouse squatting in a large bulge in the river. On its southern bank is the lock, which was built in 1892 on the site of an old weir and flash lock. At its northern end is a small weir, which because the island widens at its downstream end, helps form a stunningly beautiful lagoon. Not surprisingly this is a popular place for mooring boats and picnicking.

Old Father Thames at St John's Island, Lechlade.

A little way along are the **Radcot Aits**. These two large islands fill a big oblong bulge in the river creating three separate channels, the central one separating the two islands. Both islands were created in 1787 when a cut was made between them to bypass the meander bend around them. Both islands are uninhabited and are almost completely open grassland with a few clumps of trees. The southern island is the larger of the two and is crossed at its upstream end by the thirteenth-century Radcot Bridge, thought to be the oldest surviving bridge over the Thames. A Saxon charter mentions the presence of a bridge here in AD958. At the downstream tip is the little Cradle footbridge to the mainland. Boats are moored along both islands' banks and they are popular destinations for campers.

A short distance around a very sharp bend is **Grafton Eyot**. This little banana-shaped island sits in the middle of the river with the lock on its northern bank and a small weir on its western tip. The lock, one of the last to be built on the Thames, and its very attractive keeper's cottage were built in 1896. The weir is on the other side of the island at the upstream end. Set in another lonely and relatively inaccessible place, this is a wonderful destination to watch for otters, as they have recently returned to this stretch of the river after an absence of many decades.

Around several more bends, passing Kelmscot Manor – the country home of William Morris – there is the haunt of a famous Thames-side ghost, the Headless Boatman. Sometime in the late 1500s, a local boatman was accused of stealing sheep and was beheaded on the riverbank by the accusing farmer. His ghost has haunted this stretch of the river ever since. Around now the Thames enters its infancy, so eloquently noted by William Morris: 'What better place than this then could we find, By this sweet stream that knows not of the sea, This little stream whose hamlets scarce have names, This far off lonely mother of the Thames.' Here the Thames divides into one large and two lesser streams, with a weir stretching across the meadow bank to **Brandy Island** and **Buscot Lock Island**.

Oblong-shaped, uninhabited Brandy Island and its neighbouring lock island lie in an idyllic setting. The diminutive streams that divide the islands tumble over their sluices in unbroken waterfalls and the views of Brandy Island and adjacent St Mary's church are prized by walkers on the Thames Path. Brandy Island takes up a fair chunk of the river and at its upstream end a weir dams the delightful tree-lined inner channel.

When Australian gold trader Robert Campbell bought nearby Buscot Park in 1859, he initiated a programme of agricultural industrialisation that included dredging the river below the lock and building two waterwheels to pump water into reservoirs that were used to irrigate the fields via a system of brick-lined drainage channels. He also built a distillery on the island for making spirit from sugar beet, hence the name Brandy Island. He even constructed a small railway to take the beet from the fields to the distillery close to Buscot Lock. The 'brandy', however, didn't prove very popular and the Buscot estate was eventually bequeathed to the National Trust in 1956.

Brandy Island itself remained under the ownership of Thames Water until October 2009, when it was sold, amid much local protest, for recreational and commercial development. This once beautiful, peaceful island, an untouched wilderness habitat for wildlife and fauna, has now sadly been cleared by bulldozers and diggers to make way for the development of the island into a boat storage yard with camping facilities.

The little Buscot Lock Island is triangular in shape and well wooded, with a new weir built in 1979. It can be reached at its upstream end from the adjacent Buscot Lock, the smallest lock on the Thames, which was opened in 1791.

After several more tortuous bends we arrive close to the end of the navigable Thames, at the last island in the river: **St John's Island**. St John's Island is the last lock on the river and also the highest lock on the Thames, at 250ft above sea level. The lock was built in 1770. It is in fact two islands joined by a small weir bridge. The first long, narrow island is the larger, and is bisected by St John's Bridge, built in 1229; it vies with Radcot Bridge for the title of the oldest on the Thames. It is a very appealing island with a path leading down the centre to picnic tables, attractive trees and the sounds of tumbling water. The second islet is prettily landscaped and is the actual lock island. St. John's Lock was first constructed in 1789.

It is befitting to end our island journey here where Rafaelle Monti's statue of Old Father Thames reclines by the lock side. The statue, built for the Great Exhibition in London in 1857, once stood beside the source of the Thames in Gloucestershire but was moved here in 1974 to protect it from vandalism.

NOTES

1 Winn, C., *I Never Knew That About the River Thames* (Ebury Press, 2010) p.49

2 Rymers are removable wooden posts slotted into a horizontal base fixed to the riverbed that holds removable timber paddles in position. These are stacked vertically and when the paddles are withdrawn, the rymers are moved aside to make an opening in the weir

CONCLUSION

THE COURSE OF this book has taken us along the length of the River Thames, from the expanse of the estuary, following salty tidal water through London, on up to the crystal-clear stream that disappears into a Cotswold meadow. Within the contours of this remarkable river lie approximately 190 islands, some so small that they hardly warrant a mention, others relatively large, hived off from the mainland in order to ease navigation. While almost two thirds of the islands are uninhabited by humans, they are nevertheless home to myriad creatures, birds and wildfowl. The islands form an important thread of habitat continuity, speckling the river's surface and providing an often completely natural wildlife refuge free from human disturbance.

Approximately 40,000 people live on the Thames islands. Aside from Canvey Island, which accounts for 37,000 of them, there are roughly 3,000 people who actually live on a Thames island. These people are a very select group. There is something secretive, illusive, intimate and comforting about all small islands and no doubt many people experience a thrill at being surrounded by water, cut off from the trials of the mainland. Witness how the Greek islands are infinitely more popular as a tourist destination than the far more interesting and beautiful mainland. An island is of a scale that is easy to comprehend, a safe and defensible space secure from the uncertain world beyond. Thus, the peace and tranquillity of these willow-shrouded sanctuaries provides a wonderful contrast to the chaos and intrusiveness of modern life.

Thames island living attracts those looking for a peaceful, alternative lifestyle and for the island communities it is indeed a unique way of life. As we have seen, islanders have to overcome some serious difficulties for the pleasure and rewards of living on an island. Life on a Thames island may be idyllic during spring and summer, but there is always the risk of fire unattended by the emergency services,

and winters can be harsh with regular floods and dangerous and unpredictable access to homes. Often those who buy into the 'dream', sell up after their first winter.

Although island communities tend to be a little introverted, as individuals the Thames islanders are incredibly open and friendly, emotions they are able to balance with a common desire to protect their 'precious privacy'. In travelling the course of the river, I was surprised at how little interconnection and communication there was between the inhabited islands. I had assumed there would be much to-ing and fro-ing between islands, with perhaps the odd competitive event between them, but surprisingly there appears to be little or no contact between the inhabitants of different islands. This applies even to those who are very near neighbours, such as Ash and Tagg's Islands.

I have often been asked which island most appeals to me, and without hesitation, I reply Chiswick Eyot. This is, however, a purely emotive and sentimental response. Although it is neither particularly attractive scenically, nor especially important historically, this little eyot has always been my favourite Thames island. It was here in the late 1960s and early '70s that my cousin Chris and I spent many happy summers, swimming off the little pebbly beach and building secret camps in our very own 'Mekong Delta'. During school holidays, on her way to work my mother would drop us off at the island with our sandwiches and drinks and pick us up on her way home. We had to sit on towels in the back of the car because we were usually still wet from the river and the car always smelled of Thames mud. In fact the seeds of this book were sown during those long-gone days.

On a less sentimental note, for sheer presence, I would say my favourite island has to be Platt's Eyot. From the first time I saw it, I was struck by its incredible size and its intriguing industrial buildings. Once ashore, I was captivated by the secret, neglected wilderness at its western end, harbouring its profusion of meadowland flowers, birds and other wildlife. It must be hoped that some agreement will soon be reached that will secure the future of this important historical island and its remaining First World War buildings.

Also among my list of favourites is Canvey Island. What a discovery, particularly Western Canvey! The sea wall and the sheer scale of the views along the vast expanse of the estuary are deeply inspiring. Giant oil tankers drifting on the horizon, the muted colours of the marshlands, little Dutch cottages, the amazing light and of course an astonishing array of wildlife: these are the enduring images of Canvey. At the other end of the scale is little Firework Ait, rescued from abandonment and now pretty as a picture, bobbing about on Windsor's foreshore.

Naturally, there are some far less appealing islands, but I'm pleased to say only three spring to mind. The first has to be De Bohun Island at Caversham Lock. It has a dark, gloomy setting, overhanging trees on an uninviting towpath and a generally sinister atmosphere. Another island that failed to appeal was Friary Island near Old Windsor. From the mainland it is almost impossible to detect that you are crossing onto an island, and the main street with its suburban-looking houses running alongside, gives the place a very sterile atmosphere. Lastly, there is nothing especially to like about Piper's Island, lying under Caversham Bridge. The large vacuous restaurant suffocates the island and has created another sterile environment. That said, the remaining 187 islands are all attractive in their own way, with a good many nestling among some of the loveliest pastoral scenery in England. Although some are admittedly merely glorified mudflats, the majority of islands have something interesting or intriguing about them.

There is something exciting about stepping onto a new island for the first time, especially the uninhabited ones. If you do visit an island, there are two golden rules to remember. Firstly, make sure it is not privately owned, and secondly that it is not the spring nesting season for birds and wildfowl. Even when visiting outside of the nesting months, make sure to tread carefully and respect the habitat by keeping to any paths.

The River Thames has transported much of England's history along its path, and some of that history has wafted over the islands, which are part of the very fabric of the river. We have seen how some islands became sanctuaries and places of refuge during the Blitz, while many others offered poor London families the chance to escape the foul air of the city for weekends of camping by the fresh Thames waterside. Other islands, such as Monkey Island and Henley's Temple Island, became gentlemen's follies, while others became the focus of huge entrepreneurial dreams. Looking at Tagg's Island today it is almost inconceivable to imagine the popular status the island once held. The most famous Thames island, Eel Pie, had a legendry alternative, progressive cultural scene. Arguably part of the appeal of Eel Pie in the 1950s and 1960s was its unique island setting. Giant Platt's Eyot played its part in the First World War and the island at Thames Ditton will forever be associated with that most notorious of all honours brokers, Maundy Gregory.

There are islands running almost the entire length of the river, yet there are few obvious similarities between Canvey Island and St John's Island: raw uncouth Thames meets quiet genteel Thames. However, whether you are supping a cup of builder's brew at Canvey's Labworth Cafe or a cup of Earl Grey at St John's Lock, the same Thames water surrounds you. The people who live on or near the islands will undoubtedly know more about them than I have been able to discover. But if this book goes some way to promote a wider understanding and appreciation of this fascinating aspect of the River Thames, then it will have achieved its objective.

BIBLIOGRAPHY

BOOKS

Ackroyd, P., *Thames: Sacred River* (Chatto & Windus, 2007)

Baker, R., *Thameside Molesey* (Barracuda Books Ltd, 1989)

Brooking, V., *Shepperton's Island Dwellers* (Sunbury & Shepperton Local History Society, 1995)

Chaplin, P.H., *The Thames from Source to Tideway* (Whittet Books, 1982)

Clarke, G., *Down by the River – The Thames and Kennet in Reading* (Two Rivers Press, 2009)

Claxon, G.W.F., *The Creek, Sunbury-on-Thames, and its Immediate Environment* (Sunbury & Shepperton Local History Society, 1984)

Cook, A., *Cash for Honours, the Story of Maundy Gregory* (The History Press, 2008)

Cullen, T., *Maundy Gregory – Purveyor of Honours* (The Bodley Head, 1974)

Hailstone, C., 'Osiers and Grig Wheels, Lost Industries of the Thames', *The Thames Book* (Link House Publications Ltd, 1974)

Harrison, I., *The Thames from Source to Sea* (Collins, 2004)

Harwood, T.E., *Windsor Old and New* (London, 1929)

Jeremiah, J., *The Upper and Middle Thames, From Source to Reading* (Phillimore, 2007)

Jerome, J.K., *Three Men in a Boat* (J.W. Arrowsmith, 1889)

Kemplay J, *The Thames Locks* (Ronald Crowhurst, 2000)

Trimble, N. (ed.) *Life on the Thames Yesterday and Today* (Sunbury and Shepperton Local History Society: 1995)

Livingston H., *The Thames Path* (Ian Allen Publishing, 1993)

McCave F., *A History of Canvey Island* (Ian Henry Publications, 1985)

Orr V., *Fawley Temple* (Henley Royal Regatta, 1994)

Read S. (ed.) *The Thames of Henry Taunt* (Sutton Publishing, 1989)

Rolt, L.T.C., *The Thames From Mouth to Source* (B.T. Batsford Ltd, 1951)

Schneer, J., *The Thames, England's River* (Abacus, 2005)

Sinclair, M., *The Thames, A Cultural History* (Oxford University Press, 2007)

Thacker, F.S., *The Thames Highway: A General History* (1914)

Thacker, F.S., *The Thames Highway: Locks and Weirs* (1912)

Van Der Vat, D., and Whitby M., *Eel Pie Island* (Francis Lincoln Ltd, 2009)

Wilson, D.G., *The Making of the Middle Thames* (Spurbooks Ltd, 1977)

Winn C., *I Never Knew That about the River Thames* (Ebury Press, 2010)

ARTICLES

Claxton, F., 'The Creek, Sunbury-on-Thames and its immediate Environment', Sunbury and Shepperton Local History Society, 1984

Dutton, S., '"Eyots and Aits" Footnotes to Local History', *Richmond and Twickenham Times*, 5 February 1938

East, J.M., 'Karno's Folly, or How to Lose a Show-Business Fortune', *Theatre Quarterly*, July–September 1971

Pape, D., 'Nature Conservation in Hounslow' in *Ecology Handbook 15* (London Ecology Unit, 1990)

Summerville, C., 'Down By the Jetty', *Coast* magazine, April 2008

Thomas, G., 'Monkey Island', *Thames Valley Countryside*, Vol.8, No.30, Autumn 1968

Underhill, M., 'Fred Karno and the Gypsies' Curse', *Country Life*, 17 January 1908

Whitnall, F.G., 'The World's End', *Essex Countryside*, January 1967

Williams, J., 'Molesey Memories', *The Molesey Review*, August–September 1953

ISLANDS IN THE RIVER THAMES

This island list begins at the Thames estuary in Essex and ends at St John's Lock at Lechlade in Gloucestershire.

Two Tree Island
Canvey Island
Lower Horse and Upper Horse Islands
Frog Island
Chiswick Eyot
Oliver's Eyot
Brentford Ait
Lot's Ait
Isleworth Ait
The Flowerpot Islands
Corporation Island
Glover's Island
Eel Pie Island
Swan Island
Teddington Lock Ait
Angler's Ait
Trowlock Island
Steven's Eyot & Islet
Raven's Ait
Boyle Farm Island
Swan Island
Thames Ditton Island
Ash Island
Tagg's Island
Duck Ait
Garrick's Ait
Benn's Eyot
Platt's Eyot
Grand Junction Island
Sunbury Court Island
Rivermead Island
Sunbury Lock Ait

Wheatley's Ait
Desborough Island
D'Oyly Carte Island
Lock Island
Hamhaugh Island
Pharaoh's Island
Penton Hook Island
Penton Hook Lock Island
Truss Island
Church Island
Hollyhock Island
Holm Island
Hythe End Island
Magna Carta Island
Pats Croft Island
Kingfisher Island
Friary Island
Friday Island
Old Windsor Lock Island
Ham Island
Lion Island
Sumptermead Ait
Black Pott's Ait
Romney Eyot
Cutler's Ait
Firework Ait
Snap Ait
Deadwater Ait
White Lillies Island
Boveney Lock Island
Bush Ait
Queen's Eyot
Monkey Island

Pigeonhill Eyot
Bray Lock Island
Headpile Eyot
Tiny Unamed Ilet
Guards Club Ait
Bridge Eyot
Mill Ait
Grass Eyot
Glen Island
Ray Mill Island
Boulter's Island
Sloe Grove Islands or Bavin's Gulls
Formosa Island
Cookham Lock Island
Sashes Island
Gibraltar Islands
Bridge Eyot
Marlow Lock Island
Temple Mill Island
Temple Lock Island
Hurley Lock Islands
Poisson Deux Islands
Magpie Island
Hambledon Lock Islands
Temple Island
East Eyot
Rod Eyot
Marsh Lock Aits
Ferry Eyot
Poplar Eyot
Handbuck Eyot
Wargrave Marsh Island

Lashbrook Ait
Shiplake Bridge Ait
Shiplake Lock Ait
Phillimore Isand
The Lynch
Hallsmead Ait
Buck Ait & Islet
Sonning Eyots
Horden Ait
Heron Island
View Island
De Bohun Island
Fry's Island
Pipers Island
St Mary's Island
Appletree Eyot
Poplar Eyot
Roebuck Ait
Ferry Eyot
Mapledurham Eyot
Mapledurham Lock Island
Hardwick Ait
Whitchurch Mill Ait
Whitchurch Lock Ait
Hartslock Aits
Gatehampton Eyot
Grim's Ditch Eyots
Heart Eyot
Swann Eyot
Cleve Eyots
Mouslford Eyots
Benson's Eyot
Benson's Lock Island

Lock House Island
Day's Lock Island
Clifton Lock Island
Clifton Cut Island
Culham Island
Andersey Island
Nag's Head Island
Abbey Island
Abingdon Lock Island
Lock Wood Island
Sandford Eyot
Fidlers Elbow
Rose Island
Iffley Lock Island
Grand Pont Island
Osney Aits
Fiddlers Island
Medley Eyot
Godstow Lock Island
Godstow Eyot
King's Eyot
Eynsham Eyot
Swinford Eyot
Pinkhill Eyot
Northmore Eyot
Shifford Island
Rushey Lock Island
Radcot Lock Island
Radcot Aits
Grafton Eyot
Brandy Island
Buscot Lock Island
St John's Island

INDEX

Visit our website and discover thousands of other History Press books.

www.thehistorypress.co.uk